Gallery Books
Editor: Peter Fallon

WONDERFUL TENNESSEE

Brian Friel

WONDERFUL TENNESSEE

Gallery Books

Wonderful Tennessee
is first published
simultaneously in paperback
and in a clothbound edition
on the day of its première
30 June 1993.

The Gallery Press
Loughcrew
Oldcastle
County Meath
Ireland

For an extension of this copyright page
see Acknowledgements on page 93.

ISBN 1 85235 114 4 (*paperback*)
    1 85235 115 2 (*clothbound*)

    The Gallery Press receives financial assistance from An Chomhairle Ealaíon / The Arts Council, Ireland, and acknowledges also the assistance of the Arts Council of Northern Ireland in the publication of this book.

Characters

Three married couples all in their late thirties/early forties:

TERRY
BERNA
GEORGE
TRISH
FRANK
ANGELA

Terry is Trish's brother. Angela and Berna are sisters.

Time and place

The action takes place on a remote pier in north-west Donegal.
 Time — the present.

Set

A stone pier at the end of a headland on the remote coast of north-west Donegal. The stone-work is grained with yellow and grey lichen. The pier was built in 1905 but has not been used since the hinterland became depopulated many decades ago.

The pier extends across the full width of the stage. It begins stage left (the mainland) and juts out into the sea so that it is surrounded by water on three sides — the auditorium, the area stage right, and the back wall. (N.B. *Left and right from the point of view of the audience.*)

From the floor of the pier stone steps lead down to the sea/ auditorium. Steps also lead up to the cat-walk, eighteen inches wide and about five feet above the floor of the pier. From the cat-walk one can see over the back wall of the pier (about ten feet high) and right across the surrounding countryside and sea.

There are some weather-bleached furnishings lying around the pier floor: fragments of fishing-nets, pieces of lobster-pots, broken fish-boxes. Some rusty bollards and rings. A drift of sand in the top right-hand corner. Stones once used as weights inside lobster-pots. A listing and rotting wooden stand, cruciform in shape, on which hangs the remnant of a life-belt.

People can enter and exit only stage left.

Originally Produced in Dublin by The Abbey Theatre and Noel Pearson, *Wonderful Tennessee* opened at The Abbey Theatre, Dublin, on 30 June 1993, with the following cast:

ANGELA	Catherine Byrne
TRISH	Marion O'Dwyer
BERNA	Ingrid Craigie
TERRY	Donal McCann
FRANK	John Kavanagh
GEORGE	Robert Black

Director	Patrick Mason
Stage Director	Michael Higgins
Assistant Stage Director	Catriona Behan
Set and Costume Designer	Joe Vanek
Lighting Designer	Mick Hughes
Sound	David Nolan

for
D.E.S. Maxwell

ACT ONE

Scene One

A very warm day in August. Early afternoon. Silence and complete stillness.

Then after a time we become aware that there are natural sounds: the gentle heave of the sea; a passing seagull; the slap and sigh of water against the stone steps. This lasts until we have established both a place and an environment of deep tranquillity and peace.

Now we hear another sound from a long distance away — an approaching minibus, and almost as soon as we identify the sound, discrepant and abusive in this idyllic setting, fade in the sound of people singing 'Happy Days are Here Again'. Boisterous singing, raucous singing, slightly tiddley, day-excursion singing that is accompanied on the piano accordion.

Trish sings a solo line and this is greeted with laughter, mockery, cheers, encouragement. Then everybody joins in again.

Now the minibus has arrived and stops at the end of the pier (i.e. stage left off), and the idyllic atmosphere is completely shattered: doors banging; shouting; laughter; a sense of excitement and anticipation; animated, overlapping chatter.

TRISH Help! We're lost!

BERNA Where are we?

TERRY This is it.

TRISH You're lost, Terry; admit it; we're lost.

FRANK It — is — wonderful!

ANGELA This can't be it, is it?

TERRY Believe me — this is it.

TRISH Help!

> FRANK, *off, sings the title of 'Happy Days are Here Again'.*

ANGELA Where's this wonderful island? I see no island.

TRISH We're lost — we're lost — we're lost! Help!

TERRY This is where we get the boat, Trish.

TRISH Oh my God — lost!

FRANK Anybody seen my camera?

TRISH Lost — lost!

TERRY Isn't it wonderful?

FRANK Sober up, everybody, please.

ANGELA You're joking, Terry, aren't you?

TRISH Lost, I'm telling you. This is the back of nowhere.

TERRY This is it — believe me.

> GEORGE *plays: 'O Mother, I could weep for mirth / Joy fills my heart so fast'.* TRISH *sings ' — weep for mirth — ' and says:*

TRISH So could I, George.

> *And* FRANK *simultaneously sings the line, 'Joy fills my heart so fast' to* GEORGE's *accompaniment.*

BERNA Mind the step.

ANGELA Admit it, Terry: you're lost.

BERNA Here's your camera, Frank.

TRISH Let me out of here. Help!

FRANK Thanks, Berna.

TRISH I'm going straight back with you, Charlie.

ANGELA What in God's name are we doing here?

TERRY Admit it — isn't it wonderful?

TRISH Wonderful, he says! Help!

TERRY Yes, I think it's wonderful.

FRANK There's not a house within a hundred miles.

BERNA Let's all go back with Charlie.

TRISH Heeeeeeeelp!

> *Now* GEORGE *begins to play 'I Want to be Happy'. Cheers and mocking laughter at the choice. Through his playing:*

ANGELA Right, George! So do I!

TRISH Happy — here?

ANGELA Yeah-yeah-yeah-yeah! Why not?

BERNA Happy, happy, happy, happy.

FRANK Yes, George, yes.

And they join in the song and continue talking through it.

BERNA Whose sleeping-bag is this?

TRISH Mine, Berna. Thank you.

ANGELA At least we'll get a bit of sun.

TRISH Hand me that blanket, Berna.

FRANK We're the first people ever to set foot here.

BERNA Here's your sun hat, Angela.

FRANK Careful. I'm closing this door.

TRISH Help!

TERRY enters, animated, laughing, excited. Like all the others he is dressed in colourful summer clothes. He has a sleeping-bag slung over his shoulder and carries two large expensive hampers filled with food and drink. As he enters TRISH calls:

(*Off*) Is this your idea of a joke, Terry?

GEORGE stops playing.

TERRY (*On*) What's that?

TRISH (*Off*) Is this some kind of practical joke?

TERRY Believe me — it's everything you ever dreamed of.

FRANK (*Off*) Wonderful!

TERRY Believe me.

And immediately GEORGE strikes up 'I Want to be Happy' again.

Quite right, George! (*Sings*) ' — but I won't be happy / 'Till I make you happy too — '

GEORGE continues with the song; and some of the

13

people off join in the singing. But TERRY's *laughter suddenly stops. Eagerly, with a hint of anxiety, he searches out the island (at the back of the auditorium, right) and at the same time in a low, barely audible voice, he mumbles/speaks the words of the song the others are singing off.*

Now he has found the island. He drops the hampers. He slips the straw hat off his head, holds it against his chest and gazes out to sea. After a few seconds FRANK *enters. Like* TERRY *he is dressed in bright summer clothes.*

FRANK The minibus is about to —

> TERRY *is so intent on the island that he does not hear him.*

Terry, your minibus is about to head home and Charlie wants to know — (*Calls impatiently*) Please, Angela!

TERRY Look, Frank.

FRANK Turn it down, Angela, would you?

TERRY There it is.

FRANK That's a crowd of lunatics you have there. So what time tomorrow is Charlie to come back for us?

TERRY Whenever it's bright.

FRANK It'll be sort of bright all night, I hope. Let's say — what? Seven? Seven-thirty?

TERRY That's fine.

FRANK Seven-thirty okay with you?

TERRY (*Indifferently*) Fine — fine.

> *Burst of laughter off.*

FRANK Surely to God they can't keep that pace up all night!

> *As he turns to leave* BERNA *enters. Dressed for the outing and carrying a hold-all, various bags, a sleeping-bag, etc.*

BERNA (*Singing earnestly*) 'When skies are grey and you say

you are blue — '
FRANK Certainly am, Berna.

He swings her round in a dance and sings along with
her.

BOTH 'I'll send the sun shining through — '
FRANK Wow-wow-wow-wow! Hey, Terry: some mover that
lady of yours! (*Exiting*) Right, Charlie. All settled.
Seven-thirty tomorrow morning.

The moment FRANK *exits* BERNA's *brittle-bright face is*
transformed with anxiety. She goes quickly to TERRY's
side and speaks in a low, urgent voice. GEORGE *suddenly*
stops playing 'I Want to be Happy' in mid-phrase and
plays 'Jesu, Joy of Man's Desiring'.

TRISH Lovely, George.

She sings with GEORGE.

BERNA I want to go home.
TERRY There it is, Berna. Look.
BERNA Take me home, Terry — please.
TERRY Wonderful, isn't it?
BERNA Please, Terry.
TERRY Just for tonight, Berna — just one night. Believe me —
you'll love it.
BERNA Have you any idea how desperately unhappy I am?
TERRY Berna, I —
BERNA I don't think I can carry on, Terry.
TERRY Of course you can carry on. The doctor says you're a lot
better. (*He reaches out to touch her*) Did you remember
to take your pills this morning?

The music stops.

BERNA (*Quietly, almost with pity*) For God's sake . . .

She moves quickly away from him and busies herself

with her belongings. The moment she says 'For God's sake' the engine starts up. Again the overlapping voices off.

TRISH He's going.
ANGELA See you tomorrow morning.
TRISH Help!
FRANK Don't go, Charlie! Don't abandon us!
ANGELA Thank you, Charlie.
TRISH Stop him. Don't let him go!

GEORGE *begins to play 'Aloha', and this is greeted with laughter and groans and singing.*

FRANK Perfect, George!

FRANK *sings a phrase of the song.*

TRISH Come back, Charlie! Help! Come back!
ANGELA 'Bye, lovely world!

FRANK *continues singing.*

TRISH 'Bye, civilisation.
ANGELA 'Bye, Charlie.
TRISH Don't forget us, Charlie.
ALL 'Bye . . . 'bye . . . 'bye . . .

TERRY *and* BERNA *stand in silence, motionless, watching the departing bus.*

BERNA (*Softly*) 'Bye, Charlie . . . 'bye . . .

The music, the singing, the shouting all stop. The sound of the departing bus fades away. Silence. Once again the landscape is still! and totally silent. Then ANGELA, *unaccompanied and at half the song's usual tempo, belts out the defiant line.*

ANGELA (*Sings*) 'I want to be happy — '

TRISH Damn right, Angela!

ANGELA (*Sings*) 'But I won't be happy — '

TRISH Why not?

ANGELA (*Sings*) ''Till I make you happy too.'

> *And at this point she is joined first by* GEORGE *on the accordion, then by* TRISH, *and then very privately, almost inaudibly, by* BERNA.
>
> *After* ANGELA's *first line, 'I want to be happy', slowly accelerate the tempo to normal.*
>
> *Now enter — immediately after the line ''Till I make you happy too' —* GEORGE, ANGELA, FRANK *and* TRISH *(in that order); each holding on to the waist of the person in front; all (except* GEORGE) *singing lustily; all doing a clownish, parodic conga dance, heads rolling, arms flying — a hint of the maenadic. All are dressed in bright summer clothes and each carries some gaudy summer equipment — straw bags, sun hats, sleeping-bags, sun umbrellas, cameras, binoculars, etc., etc.*
>
> *Suddenly the pier becomes a fairground.*
>
> GEORGE *is the accordionist. His neck is swathed in a white bandage. On those rare occasions when he speaks his voice is husky and barely audible.* TRISH *has a plastic cup (wine) in one hand.* ANGELA *swings an empty wine bottle by the neck. The moment they come on stage* TERRY's *face lights up and happily, extravagantly he joins in the singing and the dance.*

ALL 'Life's really worth living — '

TRISH Come on, Berna! Party time!

> *And after a moment's hesitation* BERNA *joins in the parade and the singing with earnest, deliberate enthusiasm.*

ALL ' — when we are mirth-giving / Why can't I give some to you?'

> FRANK *now stands aside and takes a series of rapid photographs. Now only* TERRY *and* ANGELA *sing to*

GEORGE's *accompaniment.*

DUET 'When skies are grey — '
TRISH Terrific, Angela!
DUET ' — and you say you are blue — '
TERRY Your wife's a star, Frank.
FRANK Blessed, amn't I?
ANGELA (*Solo*) 'I'll send the sun smiling through — ' Give me
your hand, Berna! So —

*Now back to the very slow tempo and the exaggerated
steps.* ANGELA *and* BERNA, *hand in hand, dance/
promenade across the pier.*

ANGELA⎫ 'I want to be happy — '
BERNA⎭
FRANK The wonderful sisters!
ANGELA⎫ 'But I won't be happy / 'Till I make you happy too.'
BERNA⎭

ANGELA *suddenly stops and holds her head.*

ANGELA Oh God!

The music stops.

The head's beginning to reel!
FRANK (*Sings*) 'In the good old summer time — '

GEORGE *drowns* FRANK's *singing with a very formal
'Amen' cadence.*

TERRY Thank you, George.

General laughter. TERRY *holds his hands up.*

And now, my children — please.
TRISH Quiet, everybody!
TERRY Your attention, please.
FRANK Please!

TERRY I bid you all welcome.

FRANK Thank you, Terence.

TRISH Where are we, Terry?

FRANK Arcadia.

TERRY Ballybeg pier — where the boat picks us up.

TRISH County what?

TERRY County Donegal.

TRISH God. Bloody Indian territory.

FRANK Where does the boatman live?

TERRY Back there. At the end of the sand-dunes.

TRISH (*To* GEORGE) Ballybeg, George. In County Donegal.

GEORGE *nods and smiles.*

TERRY Right. So — stage one complete. Welcome again.

ANGELA Sounds proprietorial, doesn't he?

TERRY I'm only the sherpa.

TRISH Only what? (*To* BERNA) What's a sherpa?

FRANK (*Up on cat-walk*) Next parish Boston, folks!

TERRY (*Privately*) Are you alright?

ANGELA A little too much wine.

TERRY And you've changed your hair.

ANGELA For the big occasion! Of course!

TERRY Lovely.

> *She touches his shoulder quickly, lightly, and moves away. They deposit their belongings at various places along the pier — that place becomes that person's 'territory' for the rest of the night.*
>
> *Now they all move around slowly, silently, assessing the pier itself and its furnishings and the surrounding sea and countryside.* TERRY *watches them. He is anxious to have their approval.*

Well?

FRANK (*In approval*) Well-well-well-well.

TERRY So far so good?

FRANK So far wonderful, Terry.

TERRY (*To all*) Isn't it?

FRANK Wonderful.

FRANK *comes down from the cat-walk.*

TERRY Some place, George?

GEORGE Yes. Yes.

TRISH Sorry, Terry — where is this again?

FRANK (*To* TERRY) Permanently lost, that sister of yours.

TERRY Ballybeg pier.

TRISH In County — ?

FRANK Wasting your time, Terry.

TERRY Donegal. This is where the boat picks us up.

TRISH You've told me that three times. (*To* GEORGE) The boat picks us up here.

> GEORGE *nods and smiles. Pause.*
> *Again they gaze around, touching the furnishings, sitting on the bollards. As they move around* GEORGE *plays 'Jesu, Joy of Man's Desiring'.* ANGELA *busies herself with her belongings, deliberately ignoring the surroundings.*

A long time since this has been used.

TERRY Not for fifty years.

FRANK More, I'd say.

TERRY Well?

FRANK Listen! Not a sound.

TERRY Trish?

TRISH Very . . . remote, isn't it?

TERRY But worth four hours in that minibus?

TRISH (*Not quite certain*) Oh yes . . .

FRANK The bus was fine. It's Charlie's terrible jokes I can't take. If he were my driver, Terry, I'd muzzle him.

TERRY (*To* ANGELA) Some place, isn't it?

TRISH Wonderful, Terry. Isn't it, Berna?

BERNA Yes.

FRANK These (*rings*) were made to last.

TERRY And that stone — all cut by hand. (*Again attempting to include* ANGELA) What do you call that mossy stuff — lichen?

TRISH And that view! Look!

FRANK What were these stones for?

TERRY Weights for lobster-pots.

FRANK Amazing. Another world altogether.

TRISH Heavenly.

TERRY Yes.

TRISH You'd think you could see *beyond* the horizon. It really is wonderful. Oh my goodness . . . (*To* GEORGE) Ballybeg pier. In County Donegal.

GEORGE I know, Trish!

TERRY (*To* ANGELA) What do you think of it?

ANGELA 'Wonderful.' I know another happy song, George.

> ANGELA *sings the first line of the refrain of 'I Don't Know Why I'm Happy'.* GEORGE *picks it up immediately.*

Yes! He's a genius!

> *She sings the second line of the refrain.*

TERRY Your wonderful wife — off again.

FRANK (*Spreading his hands*) Your wonderful sister-in-law.

> TERRY *sings the third and fourth lines with* ANGELA.

TERRY Once more!

> *And accompanied by* GEORGE *and with* TRISH *clapping in time they sing the whole refrain again.*

Remember Father singing that every Christmas?

TRISH Don't remember that. Did he?

ANGELA Your George is a genius, Trish.

TRISH I know.

ANGELA Give me a kiss, George.

> *She kisses him.*

You should be wearing a toga and playing a lyre and gorging yourself with black grapes.

She picks up a wreath of dried seaweed and places it on his head.

There! Dionysus!

TRISH I have a suggestion, Terry: let's have the party here.

FRANK (*Holding up a fragment of the life belt*) Anybody drowning?

TERRY We have a boat coming for us, Trish.

TRISH We don't have to take it, do we?

TERRY Yes, we do.

TRISH Why?

FRANK Because it's all arranged.

TRISH Berna, what do you say?

BERNA I don't care. Here's fine. Here's wonderful.

TRISH Angela?

ANGELA I know another happy song!

FRANK (*Icily*) Angela, we're all trying to —

TERRY (*Sings*) 'Here we are again — '

ANGELA That's it!

GEORGE *picks up the melody.*

(*Sings*) 'Happy as can be — '

TRISH I know that!

TRISH, TERRY *and* ANGELA *all sing together.*

TRIO 'All good pals and jolly good company.'

ANGELA *now continues alone. She hoists up her skirts and does a parodic dance up and down the pier as she sings.* TERRY *and* TRISH *clap hands.*
ANGELA's *performance is full and exuberant but at the same time there is a hint of underlying panic.*

ANGELA (*Singing and dancing*) 'A kiss for Bernadette,
My darling sister, B.
I think I need a very strong cup of tea.'

FRANK (*Icily*) Not at all! You're wonderful!

ANGELA 'I may be slightly drunk

22

As teachers oughtn't be.
But Frank, my husband,
Tra-la-la-la-la-la-lee — '
Oh, God . . .

She flops on to a bollard.

FRANK Thank you very much. Now — what about this boat, Terry?

TRISH I vote we stay here. Berna?

FRANK Terry's day, Trish.

TRISH Aren't we all happy enough here?

ANGELA (*Sings to same air*) 'Today is Terry's day — '

FRANK (*To* TERRY) What do you say?

TERRY You think this is great? Believe me, my children, you ain't seen nuthin' yet.

ANGELA One final happy song —

FRANK For Christ's sake!

ANGELA And despite my husband's encouragement the last happy song I'll sing.

TRISH Yes, Angela, sing! Let's have a song!

ANGELA And this last happy song is for our host, Terry Martin.

TRISH My wonderful brother.

FRANK Mister Terence Martin!

TERRY Terence Mary Martin.

ANGELA Concert promoter.

TERRY She means showman.

ANGELA Turf accountant.

FRANK Yeah!

TERRY She means bookie.

ANGELA Gambler.

TERRY She means eejit.

ANGELA And a man of infinite generosity and kindness.

Overlapping voices:

GEORGE Yes!

FRANK Hear — hear!

ANGELA Yeah-yeah-yeah!

TRISH Perfectly true!

FRANK Yes!

TERRY (*Embarrassed*) That sho' is me, folks.

ANGELA (*Raising a bottle*) To Terence Mary.

TRISH To Terry and Berna.

ANGELA Friend, brother-in-law, most generous of —

> GEORGE *plays another 'Amen' chord that drowns out the rest of her speech.*

Behave yourself, you!

TERRY Wait-wait-wait-wait-wait. Give me a hand here, Frank.

> TERRY *throws open a hamper and produces bottles.*

FRANK We're not having the party here, are we?

ANGELA I want to sing another cheap song.

TERRY There are more cups in that bag.

ANGELA You sing, Berna!

BERNA Later, maybe.

TRISH It's not champagne, is it?

TERRY That's what the man sold me.

ANGELA George! A cheap song!

GEORGE We'll drink first.

TRISH Oh God, Terry!

FRANK Anybody need a cup?

TRISH A bit mad this, isn't it? What time of day is it? (*To* BERNA) Maybe we're all mad, are we?

BERNA Maybe.

FRANK May concerts and gambling and bookmaking always prosper.

TRISH Oh God, Terry, something wrong with this, isn't there?

TERRY Why?

ANGELA (*Sings*) 'Oh, Terry Martin, what can I do — '

TERRY (*Sings*) 'I took a bus to Ballybeg and I found myself with you.' Berna? (*Drink*)

BERNA Up to the top, please.

TERRY (*Softly*) You okay?

BERNA (*Loudly*) That's not the top.

TERRY Shouldn't you go easy on — ?

BERNA That's sufficient, thank you.

ANGELA (*To* FRANK) Both (*cups*) up to the brim, please.

FRANK You'll get your share.

ANGELA Jesus, how I love a prodigal man! To cheap songs!

TERRY George? (*Drink*)

GEORGE Please.

TRISH Just a little, Terry.

But GEORGE *tilts the bottle and fills his cup to over-flowing.*

GEORGE Lovely. Thanks.

TERRY Good idea this, isn't it?

TRISH We're blessed in the weather. He's (*George*) looking well, isn't he?

TERRY Great. To the old band, George.

GEORGE The Dude Ranchers.

TERRY The Dude Ranchers. The best band ever to tour Ireland. How many years were we on the road?

TRISH Twenty-one.

TERRY Were we?

GEORGE A lifetime.

TRISH A lifetime, he says.

GEORGE And we'll do it again.

TRISH You were told not to speak.

TERRY Yes, we'll do it again! And this time we'll tour the world!

GEORGE *smiles, spreads his hands and moves away.*

BERNA I'll have some more champagne, Frank.

FRANK On the way.

ANGELA (*To* BERNA) Shouldn't you go easy on that, love?

FRANK Don't spare it. Loads more in that hamper.

BERNA Thank you, Frank.

TRISH *and* TERRY *are alone.*

TERRY How is he? (*George*)

TRISH He plays all day long. As if he were afraid to stop.

TERRY He's looking great.

TRISH You've got to stop sending that huge cheque every week, Terry.

TERRY Nothing. It's —

TRISH We can manage fine.

TERRY It's only —

TRISH We don't need it. Honestly.

TERRY How was the check-up last week?

TRISH Three months at most.

TERRY Oh, Christ. Does he know?

TRISH He's very brave about it.

TERRY Is there anything — ?

TRISH (*Aloud*) Quiet, please! The brother is going to make a speech!

TERRY The brother is — !

FRANK Speech! Silence! Speech!

TERRY The brother is going to do nothing —

FRANK Glasses all full?

Overlapping talk.

Any more champagne?

TRISH Listen to the brother.

ANGELA Good man, Terry.

TRISH Go ahead.

FRANK Please! Quiet!

TRISH And make it short, Terry.

ANGELA Terence Mary Martin!

FRANK But first — first — may I say something? To Terry, for whom we all have the utmost respect and affection, and to his lovely Berna, both of whom have made all our lives —

ANGELA (*Quickly, lightly*) Happy birthday.

FRANK A very happy —

> *And the rest is drowned by* GEORGE *playing 'Happy Birthday to You'. And everybody joins in the singing.*
>
>   TERRY *covers his face in exaggerated but genuine embarrassment and pretends to hide behind the life-belt stand while they sing to him. When the chorus ends he sings the first two lines of the refrain of 'I'm*

Twenty-one Today'.
General laughter.

TRISH Alright, Terry. One very short speech.
TERRY No-no-no-no-no. No speeches. May I have your attention, please? Berna? George?
FRANK Attention, please.
TERRY Okay?

> *They all fall silent.* TERRY *points out to sea. They line up around him —* FRANK, TRISH, BERNA, GEORGE. ANGELA *moves off and stands alone.*

Straight out there. That island. That's where we're going.
FRANK Yes . . .
TRISH I'm lost — where? — Is it — ?
FRANK Wonderful . . .
TERRY (*To* TRISH) Directly in front of you.
FRANK Further left, Trish.
TERRY (*To* BERNA) Straight out there.
BERNA I see it, Terry.
FRANK (*To* TRISH) Got it?
TRISH Think so . . .
TERRY George?
GEORGE See it.
TERRY See it, Angela?

> *She does not answer.*

FRANK That's no distance out, Terry.
TERRY I suppose not.
TRISH It's shaped like a ukulele, is it?
FRANK That's a perfect circle for God's sake.
TERRY So. There we are. See it, Angela? Our destination.
ANGELA (*Softly; toasting*) Our 'destination'.
TRISH I do see it. Yes.
TERRY Wonderful, isn't it?
BERNA It's not circular, Frank. That's a rectangle.
TRISH God, that's miles away, Terry.

TERRY Is it?

TRISH Miles. And that's in County Sligo too, isn't it?

FRANK Jesus.

TERRY Donegal.

TRISH Ah.

TERRY Wonderful, isn't it?

ANGELA (*Softly; toasting*) A destination of wonder.

FRANK (*Coldly*) Aren't you going to join us, Angela?

TRISH (*To* GEORGE) Not Sligo, George. Still Donegal.

> ANGELA *stands beside the life-belt stand, leans against it, and sings in Marlene Dietrich style the first line of 'Falling in Love Again'.*

FRANK Angela, please —

> GEORGE *accompanies her now. She sings the next two lines and breaks off suddenly.* GEORGE *finishes the verse and then stops.*
>   *Silence again as they all — except* ANGELA — *gaze out at the island, each with his/her thoughts.*
>   ANGELA *takes off her sun hat and hangs it on the arm of the life-belt stand.*

TRISH You never said it was a big island, Terry.

TERRY It's not big, is it?

TRISH That's a huge island.

TERRY Is it?

FRANK Hard to know what size it is — it keeps shimmering.

> *Now for the first time* ANGELA *joins them and looks out to sea.*

ANGELA Has it a name, our destination?

TERRY Oileán Draíochta. What does that mean, all you educated people?

TRISH That rules me out. Where's our barrister? (*Berna*)

BERNA Island of Otherness; Island of Mystery.

TRISH God, it's not spooky, Terry, is it?

BERNA Not that kind of mystery. The wonderful — the sacred

— the mysterious — that kind of mystery.

FRANK Good girl, Berna!

TRISH All the same it's beautiful. (*To* GEORGE) Isn't it?

GEORGE Yes.

TRISH Damnit, I've lost it again. (*To* TERRY) You're sure it's not a mirage?

FRANK *catches her head and turns it.*

FRANK You're looking away beyond it.

TRISH Am I?

TERRY There *is* a legend that it was once a spectral, floating island that appeared out of the fog every seven years and that fishermen who sighted it saw a beautiful country of hills and valleys, with sheep browsing on the slopes, and cattle in green pastures, and clothes drying on the hedges. And they say they saw leaves of apple and oak, and heard a bell and the song of coloured birds. Then, as they watched it, the fog devoured it and nothing was seen but the foam swirling on the billow and the tumbling of the dolphins.

TRISH Will we see dolphins? God, I love dolphins.

ANGELA You know that by heart.

TERRY (*Embarrassed*) Do I?

BERNA When did it stop being spectral?

TERRY On one of its seven year appearances fishermen landed on it and lit a fire.

FRANK What was wrong with that?

TERRY Fire dispels the enchantment — according to the legend. (*To* ANGELA) You're right. From a pamphlet about the place my father had.

FRANK Maybe it is a bit like a ukulele.

TERRY Nearly forgot — shoes off, everybody!

FRANK What?

TERRY We're supposed to be barefoot.

FRANK You're joking, Terry!

TRISH Why barefoot?

TERRY Don't ask me. That's the custom. That's what people used to do long ago.

They slip out of their shoes. And again they gaze out to sea.

BERNA There are bushes on it.

FRANK Come on, Berna! And clothes drying on the hedges?

BERNA Whins, I think. Yes; they're whins. And a small hill away to the left.

TRISH God, you've all powerful eyes.

FRANK Looks more like clouds to me.

BERNA A low hill. At the end of that side.

ANGELA (*To* TERRY) You're our expert. Is there a hill there?

TERRY Expert! I was there just once with my father. I was only seven at the time.

TRISH I never heard that story.

TERRY We fasted from the night before, I remember. And for the night you were on the island you were given only bread and water. (*To* GEORGE) Like some of our digs when we were on the road!

> GEORGE *nods and smiles.* FRANK *now takes a series of photographs — of the others, of the island, of the furnishings of the pier.*

TRISH And what did you do out there?

TERRY I don't remember a lot. There were three beds — you know, mounds of stone — and every time you went round a bed you said certain prayers and then picked up a stone from the bottom of the mound and placed it on the top.

FRANK Trish! (*Photograph*)

TRISH Oh, Frank!

TERRY And I remember a holy well, and my father filling a bottle with holy water and stuffing the neck with grass — you know, to cork it. And I remember a whin bush beside the well —

TRISH There! Good for you, Berna!

TERRY And there were crutches and walking-sticks hanging on the bush; and bits of cloth — *bratóga*, my father called them — a handkerchief, a piece of a shawl — bleached and turning green from exposure. Votive

	offerings — isn't that the English word? And there's the ruins of a Middle Age church dedicated to Saint Conall. (*To* FRANK) Isn't that the period you're writing your book about?
FRANK	Something like that. Close enough.
TRISH	But it's not a pilgrimage island now?
TERRY	No, no; that all ended years and years ago.
TRISH	Why?
FRANK	People stopped believing, didn't they?
TERRY	Nobody does that sort of thing nowadays, do they? And when the countryside around here was populated, apparently they made *poitín* out there — that wouldn't have helped the pilgrimage business. There were even stories of drunken orgies.
ANGELA	(*Salute*) Saint Dionysus.
TRISH	But years ago people went there to be cured?
BERNA	To remember again — to be reminded.
TRISH	To remember what?
FRANK	George! (*Photograph*)
BERNA	To be in touch again — to attest.
FRANK	Angela! (*Photograph*)
TERRY	People went there just to make a pilgrimage, Trish.
FRANK	And to see apparitions. Patricia! (*Photograph*)
TRISH	But you saw crutches on that bush. So people must have been cured there.
FRANK	Apparitions were commonplace in the Middle Ages. Saint Conall must have seen hundreds of apparitions in his day. Terry! (*Photograph*)
TRISH	Don't be so cheap, Frank.
FRANK	Thousands maybe.
TRISH	(*To* TERRY) Do you believe people were cured there?
TERRY	All I know is that at seven years of age just to get sitting up all night was adventure enough for me. The first time I ever saw the dawn. I remember my head was giddy from want of sleep.
TRISH	And Father?
FRANK	Berna! (*Photograph*)
TRISH	Why did Father go out there? He believed in nothing.
FRANK	You're beautiful.
TRISH	Why did Father go out there?

FRANK For God's sake, Trish! That was another age. To pray — to do penance —

BERNA To acknowledge — to make acknowledgement.

TERRY You had another word, Berna — to attest!

GEORGE *makes a sound.*

What's that, George?

TRISH To attest to the mystery, he says.

TERRY And why not! (*Laughs*) I'm a bookie for God's sake. All I know is: that's where we'll have our party tonight. Okay?

ANGELA Once when the Greek god, Dionysus, was going to the island of Naxos he was captured by pirates who took him to be a wealthy prince —

FRANK You'd never guess. My wife teaches Classics.

ANGELA But suddenly his chains fell away, and vines and ivy sprouted all over the pirate ship, and the sailors were so frightened they jumped into the sea and turned into dolphins.

TRISH Will we really see dolphins? God, I love dolphins.

FRANK *is now up on the cat-walk.*

FRANK Where does our boat come from?

TERRY A house just across there. (*To* ANGELA) You know *that* by heart.

FRANK No house. No boat. Nothing from here to Boston except a derelict church — without a roof.

TRISH I'm sure it's very beautiful out there. But I'd be happy to settle for this. But if you all . . .

Silence as they gaze out again. Then suddenly ANGELA *leaps on top of a bollard, flings her hands above her head and proclaims in the style of an American evangelist.*

ANGELA There it is, friends — Oileán Draíochta, our destination! Wonderful — other — mysterious! Alleluia! So I ask you to join with me in that most beautiful song,

'Heavenly Sunshine'. Brother George?

As GEORGE *plays a brief introduction:*

Now — open your minds, your lungs, your arms, your hearts. All together, brothers and sisters (*Sings*) 'Heavenly sunshine, heavenly sunshine — ' Can't hear you, friends. 'Flooding my soul with glory divine — '

TERRY *now joins her.*

DUET 'Heavenly sunshine, heavenly sunshine,
Alleluia, Jesus is mine.'
ANGELA And one more time! Sister Tricia, Sister Berna — ?

TERRY, TRISH, BERNA *and* ANGELA *all together:*

ALL 'Heavenly sunshine, heavenly sunshine,
Flooding my soul with glory divine,
Heavenly sunshine, heavenly sunshine,
Alleluia, Jesus is mine — '
ANGELA And one more time, Brother George —

But instead of a reprise — and without a break in his playing — GEORGE *goes straight into 'Knees-up, Mother Brown'. This is greeted with laughter, cheers, derision — voices overlapping.*

George!
FRANK Wonderful!
TRISH Good man, George!
TERRY Sing it, Angela!
BERNA I know that one!

And they all — except GEORGE *— dance around the pier and sing the chorus at the top of their voices. When they get to the end of the chorus:*

TERRY One more time!

And again they sing the chorus. Just before it ends
FRANK *shouts:*

FRANK Quiet, please! Shut up, will you?

They fall silent.

We have a problem, good brethren. I'm telling you —
there is no boat.
ANGELA Who's for a quick drink?

TRISH *nods: Yes.*

FRANK And not only is there no boat, there isn't a house
within a hundred miles of us.
ANGELA (*To* TRISH) Champagne?

TRISH *nods.*

TRISH (*To* FRANK) Use these (*binoculars*).
TERRY Yes, there is, Frank. Just beyond the sand-dunes.

ANGELA *sings to the air of 'Abide With Me'.*

ANGELA 'Beyond the sand-dunes / You will find our boat — '
FRANK Nothing but bogland from here to the mountains. And
not a boat from here to the horizon.
TERRY A thatched cottage — further to your left.
FRANK Sorry.
TRISH You're the one with the eyes, Berna.
TERRY As far as I remember it's down at the very edge of the
water.
FRANK Hold on . . . yes . . . is that not a byre?
TERRY They're the people who do the ferrying.
FRANK Deserted, Terry. And there's grass growing out of the
thatch.
TERRY Carlin's the name. Been there for generations.
ANGELA (*Holding up a bottle*) Berna?

BERNA *signals: No.*

FRANK   Hold on . . . wait . . . Yes, you're right! There's smoke coming out of the chimney! God, that's a hovel! (*He comes down*) Right, I'll go and get Carlin. Are we all set to leave?

TERRY   Think so. Aren't we?

FRANK   And he picks us up on the island tomorrow morning — when? About seven?

TERRY   That's the plan.

FRANK   Right.

ANGELA (*Sings air of 'Abide With Me'*) 'That is the place / That shapes our destiny — '

As FRANK *passes behind her:*

FRANK   (*Privately*) You're making a nuisance of yourself.

ANGELA *sings the title of the song 'I Don't Know Why I'm Happy'.*

What if Carlin isn't at home?

TRISH   Or refuses to ferry bowsies.

ANGELA Or is dead.

FRANK   Seriously. What if — ?

TERRY   Someone from the house will take us, Frank. They've been ferrying people for thousands of years.

FRANK   I'm sure they have. All I'm asking is: supposing there is nobody free now to —

TERRY   (*Sharply, impatiently*) Tell him the new owner of the island sent you for him!

He stops short; tries to laugh.

I didn't mean to . . . ('*Let that out*' *is unsaid*)

Pause.

TRISH   Well, aren't you a close one, Terry Martin!

TERRY   I'm sorry. I —

TRISH   You kept that a big secret.

FRANK   You've actually bought Oileán Draíochta?

TERRY Four months ago. Sight unseen. Ridiculous, isn't it?

ANGELA So it's your island we're going to?

TERRY Stupid, I know. Heard by accident it was on the market. (*To* ANGELA) Miles from anywhere — good for nothing, isn't it?

ANGELA *spreads her hands.*

ANGELA Challenge for a sherpa.

TERRY I know it's ridiculous. I know it sounds —

FRANK This is no mystery tour he's taking us on — he's taking us home! Wonderful, Terry!

TRISH And I wish you luck with it. Congratulations. (*To* BERNA) So you own your own island, Mrs Martin. Very posh.

BERNA It's news to me.

TERRY I was going to tell you all out there tonight — tomorrow morning — whenever. Anyhow . . . (*To* FRANK) Will you get Carlin for us?

FRANK I'm away. Well done. Terrific!

FRANK *goes off.* TERRY *feels that some further explanation is necessary.*

TERRY Haven't seen it for over thirty years . . . and I was always curious to have another look at it . . . obsessed in a kind of way . . . and the fact that it came on the market . . .

TRISH Good. Great.

They drift apart and attend to their belongings. TERRY *goes to* TRISH.

All I can say is — you have money to burn.

TERRY Not true at all, I'm afraid.

TRISH Berna seems in better form.

TERRY Do you think so?

TRISH Plenty of chat out of her in the minibus.

TERRY She's really most content when she's in the nursing home.

TRISH (*Very softly*) Mother was right, you know: if you didn't spoil her so much.

TERRY Trish! (*To* GEORGE) Met an old friend of yours in London last week — Michael Robinson.

TRISH You never did! (*To* GEORGE) He met Michael Robinson in London, George. (*To* TERRY) And how was he?

TERRY Great . . . fine . . . well, not so good. Bumped into him in a pub. Didn't recognise him — not that I ever knew him well. Actually I thought he was a down-and-out touching me.

TRISH Michael?

TERRY I know — awful. Asking very warmly for you (*George*). Talked for over an hour about you and him at college together . . . doing your degree . . . and the duets you used to play —

TRISH Sonatas.

TERRY That's it — sonatas.

TRISH Beethoven sonatas.

TERRY Talked for over an hour. Couldn't shut him up. Eventually I gave him some money and just . . . walked away.

GEORGE *moves away and sits on a bollard.*

TRISH That's all they did for three whole years at college — play piano and violin sonatas — day and night. The Aeolians — that's what they called themselves.

TERRY He said you talked about going professional.

GEORGE Maybe . . .

TRISH They were the stars of the college. Oh such stars they were. Michael was going to be Ireland's first great concert violinist. He could have been, too. And there was absolutely no doubt that George was the new Rachmaninoff — no doubt at all about that. And together they were so brilliant, especially in the Beethoven sonatas. Oh I can't tell you how brilliant they were . . . Michael Robinson . . . oh my goodness . . .

Pause. BERNA *hums the line 'O Mother, I could weep for mirth' and stops suddenly.*

37

TERRY   (*To* ANGELA) I know you think it's crass.

ANGELA   What's that?

TERRY   Bookie Buys Island Sight Unseen.

ANGELA   But an island remembered, however vaguely.

TERRY   I did it on impulse. In memory of my father, maybe.

ANGELA   A new venue for rock concerts, wrestling matches?

TERRY   Why not? Bull fights, revivalist meetings. I was afraid you mightn't come this morning.

ANGELA   Terry Martin Productions! Dionysan Nights On Oileán Draíochta!

TERRY   If you hadn't come I'd have called it off.

ANGELA   Celebrate The Passions That Refuse To Be Domesticated!

TERRY   I would have —

ANGELA   Nature Over Culture! Instinct Over Management!

TERRY   Angela —

ANGELA   A Hymn To The Forces That Defy Civilisation!

TERRY   Oh God, Angela —

ANGELA   (*Passionately, urgently*) Please, Terry — for Christ's sake — please, not now — not now!

BERNA *stands on a fish-box and proclaims:*

BERNA   Lord, it is good for us to be here!

ANGELA   Amen to that, sister!

TERRY   Careful, Berna. That box is rotten.

BERNA   I want to sing a hymn.

ANGELA   Yes! Sing your hymn, Berna!

BERNA *now sings, her face frozen in a fixed and desperate smile.*

BERNA   'O Mother, I could weep for mirth —'

TERRY   Berna —

BERNA   'Joy fills my heart so fast —' Help me, George!

ANGELA   Help her, George.

BERNA   I'll start again. Give me a note.

GEORGE *gives her a chord.*

Thank you. 'O Mother, I could weep for mirth / Joy fills my heart so fast — '

ANGELA now sings with her.

DUET 'My soul today is heaven on earth, / O could the transport last.'

TRISH Good girl, Berna!

Now TRISH joins them.

TRIO 'I think of thee and what thou art — '

Now TERRY joins them.

QUARTET 'Thy majesty, thy state.
And I keep singing in my heart,
Immaculate! Immaculate!'

End of Scene One.

ACT ONE

Scene Two

Before the lights come up we hear GEORGE *playing the entire first verse of 'Oft in the Stilly Night'.*

About twelve hours later — the early hours of the following morning. The pier is lit by a midsummer night glow that illuminates with an icy, surreal clarity. The boisterous, day-excursion spirit has long ago evaporated. Waiting for the boat has made them weary and a bit irritable. Each has retreated into his/her own privacy and does not wish to be intruded on.

ANGELA *is sitting on a bollard, gazing without interest through the binoculars in the general direction of the island.* TRISH *is sitting with her back to the pier wall, her arms round her legs, her face on her knees.* FRANK *is on the cat-walk and looking towards Carlin's house.* BERNA *is sitting on the edge of the pier (stage right), her legs hanging over the edge of the pier floor.* GEORGE *is sitting on a fish-box, head back, eyes closed, body erect and tense, playing the last bars of the song.* TERRY *looks casually through the hampers, examining the contents, tidying up, killing time.*

The music ends.

TERRY Anybody for a slice of melting birthday-cake?

No answer. He continues tidying. Pause.

Glass of flat champagne?

No answer. He continues tidying. Pause.

Venison and Apricot Compôte? Honey Gateau? Ever hear of Honey Gateau?
TRISH Give our heads peace, Terry, would you?

40

TERRY Maybe I should bring this cake over to Carlin. Might soften his bark.

FRANK Hey-hey-hey-hey-hey! Look at that! There's smoke coming from the chimney again!

TRISH (*Wearily*) Wonderful.

FRANK He lets the fire die at midnight and then three hours later he lights it up again. What the hell is Mr Carlin up to?

TRISH We could do with a fire. It's got chilly.

FRANK What sort of a game is he playing with us?

TERRY Time has no meaning for a man like that. (*He holds up a small box*) Cherry and Mandarin Chartreuse — ? (*To* TRISH) Sorry.

> Pause. GEORGE *now plays the full chorus of 'Down by the Cane-brake'. He plays very softly and more slowly than the song is scored. His arrangement with its harmonium-style chords endows the song with the tone and dignity of a hymn. It sounds almost sacred.*
> *Immediately after he plays 'Down by the cane-brake, close by the mill,' ANGELA looks at him.*

ANGELA 'Down by the Cane-brake.'

GEORGE Know it?

ANGELA Haven't heard it in years.

TERRY What's a cane-brake?

ANGELA Shelter-belt of canes, I suppose. Protection against the elements.

TERRY Ah.

FRANK If he's not playing some sort of bizarre game with us, then explain why he lights his fire at three in the morning.

ANGELA He just loves tormenting us.

TRISH The poor man's cold, Frank.

FRANK Not that man. That man has no human feelings.

ANGELA Maybe he wants to dispel the enchantment.

TERRY Marrons Glacés — whatever they are. George?

GEORGE No, thanks.

FRANK He has betrayed us, the bastard.

TERRY He'll come, Frank. Believe me.

TRISH   We could do with a cane-brake here.

FRANK   If he never had any intention of ferrying us across —
         fine! Say that straight out! 'Sorry, bowsies, no ferrying
         today.'

TERRY   He'll come.

TRISH   Couldn't we rent his boat from him and row ourselves
         out?

FRANK   Where's the boat? Has he got a boat?

TERRY   (*To* TRISH) He'd never allow that.

TRISH   Why not?

TERRY   That's his job.

TRISH   Too late to go out now anyway.

TERRY   It's only ten to three. We'll still make it — believe me.

TRISH   Of course when I proposed we spend the night here, I
         was shouted down. Perverse — that's what you are.

FRANK   'Give me a while at the turf, Sir. That's all I need.' And
         four hours later, 'A mouthful of tea and I'll be over
         behind you'.

TRISH   Maybe he's past ferrying people. Is he very old?

FRANK   Ancient; and filthy; and toothless. And bloody smiling
         all the time.

ANGELA   Forget Mr Carlin, my darlings. Put Mr Carlin out of
         your thoughts.

FRANK   God, I always hated peasants.

TRISH   And bloody Sligo peasants are the worst, I'm sure.

TERRY   He'll come. Believe me. He'll come.

ANGELA   'Believe me — believe me — ' I suppose it's enviable in
         a way. Is it?

TERRY   What is?

She does not answer. She goes to BERNA *at the end of the
pier.*

ANGELA   What's the water like?

BERNA   Warm. Warmish.

ANGELA   Wouldn't mind a swim. Brighten us all up.

She hugs BERNA *quickly.*

And how's the baby sister?

BERNA *shrugs.*

You're looking much stronger.

BERNA Am I?

ANGELA Terry says you'll be back in the practice in a month.

BERNA That's not true. Who's looking after the children tonight?

ANGELA The McGuires next door.

BERNA The whole brood?

ANGELA I know. Hearts of gold.

BERNA I have a birthday present for young Frankie. I'll drop it in at the weekend.

ANGELA You have that godson of yours spoiled.

BERNA No, I'll get Terry to leave it in. The godson has got very . . . tentative with me recently.

ANGELA You couldn't make that —

BERNA I make him uneasy. You know how intuitive children are. I think maybe I frighten him.

ANGELA Frankie's dying about you, Berna.

BERNA 'Frighten' is too strong. When I reach out to touch him he shrinks away from me. I . . . disquiet him. Anyhow. Do you really think I look stronger?

ANGELA I know you are.

BERNA Terry thinks the reason for my trouble is that we couldn't have a child. That's what he tells the doctors. And that never worried me all that much. But it's an obsession with him. He's even more neurotic than Trish about not having children. A Martin neurosis, I tell him.

ANGELA Shhh.

BERNA And he would have been so good with children. Married the wrong sister, didn't he?

ANGELA Berna —

BERNA Oh, yes; oh, yes. When you married Frank a little portion of him atrophied. Then he turned to me. I'm the surrogate.

ANGELA You've got to —

BERNA Are you happy, Angela?

ANGELA (*Hums*) 'Happy days are here again.'

BERNA There are times when I feel I'm . . . about to be happy.

That's not bad, is it? Are you laughing at me?

ANGELA Of course I'm not laughing at you.

BERNA Maybe that's how most people manage to carry on —
'about to be happy'; the real thing *almost* within grasp,
just a step away. Maybe that's the norm. But then there
are periods — occasions — when just being alive is
. . . unbearable.

TERRY Marinated Quail and Quince Jelly. God!

TRISH The delights of the world — you have them all there.

ANGELA There are times when all of us —

BERNA He has no happiness with me — Terry. Not even
'about to be' happiness. He should leave me. I
wouldn't mind if he did. I don't think I'd mind at all.
Because in a way I feel I've moved beyond all that.

She stands up.

But then what would he do, where would he go?

She moves away. ANGELA *picks up the binoculars.*

TERRY Six months ago there was a horse called Quince Fruit
running at Cheltenham. Worst mistake of my whole
life. Practically cleaned me out, Quince Fruit almost
ruined me.

Pause. Now BERNA *begins singing the verse of 'Down
by the Cane-brake'. Immediately* GEORGE *accompanies
her. She sings in the mood* GEORGE *established earlier,
softly, quietly, but not quite as slowly as* GEORGE *played
the chorus. She tells the story of the song with intimacy
and precision, as do the others when they sing or join in,
each singing in the same quiet, internal, personal way.*

BERNA 'Down by the cane-brake, close by the mill
There lived a blue-eyed girl by the name of Nancy
Dill — '

TERRY (*To* TRISH) Mother's song.

She nods.

BERNA 'I told her that I loved her, I loved her very long,
I'm going to serenade her and this will be my song —'

TRISH now sings the chorus with BERNA.

DUET 'Come, my love, come, my boat lies low,
She lies high and dry on the O-hi-o.
Come, my love, come, and come along with me
And I'll take you back to Tennessee.'

A very brief bridging passage by GEORGE. Then TERRY sings alone.

TERRY 'Down by the cane-brake some happy day
You'll hear a wedding-bell a-ringing mighty gay.
I'm going to build a cabin and in a trundle bed
There'll be a blue-eyed baby and all because you said —'

Chorus sung by FRANK, BERNA, TRISH and TERRY. Then TRISH alone:

TRISH 'Down by the cane-brake, that's where I'll stay,
Longside of Nancy Dill 'till we are laid away.
And when we get to heaven and Peter lets us in
I'll start my wings a-flappin' and sing to her again —'

Chorus sung by FRANK, BERNA, TRISH, TERRY and ANGELA. Then a final cadence from GEORGE. Brief pause.

What time is it?
TERRY Just after three.
TRISH Night, everybody. See you in the morning. 'Bye.

Again they all retreat into their privacies. ANGELA looks through the binoculars. TERRY passes behind her. As he does:

TERRY Tennessee still there?

45

ANGELA Lost it again.
TERRY Still there. 'Believe me.'

She shrugs and smiles. TERRY *looks around at them all.*
Then he addresses them:

I know — I'm sorry — it's a mess. And when we were
planning it, it seemed a wonderful idea. It still is a
wonderful idea. And there's still a good chance we'll
make it — a very good chance. Carlin *will* come. I
honestly . . . Anyhow . . . sorry, sorry . . .

Pause.

TRISH (*Sits up*) I know when I was in Sligo before! Seventeen
years ago — at a bridge congress.
TERRY Donegal, Trish.
TRISH No, Sligo. At the old Great Southern Hotel. My partner
was a man —
FRANK Here he comes! There he is! Look! Look!
TRISH What? — Who? —
FRANK The boatman! Carlin! With his boat! He's here! He's
bloody here!

Suddenly everybody is excited, agitated. They all talk at
the same time.

TRISH Who's here?
TERRY Carlin.
BERNA Oh God.
TERRY Where is he?
TRISH Who's Carlin?
ANGELA I don't believe it.
TERRY Great — terrific! Are you sure, Frank?
BERNA (*Anxious, agitated*) Oh God! — Oh my God!
ANGELA The bastard — where is he?
TRISH Where, Frank? Where?
ANGELA I don't believe it.
BERNA Oh my God!
TERRY Is he alone? Quiet, please!

BERNA Oh my God, Angela —

TERRY Where is he, Frank?

TRISH Can you see him?

ANGELA I don't believe it.

TERRY Where is he, Frank?

FRANK 'Wolf!' cried the naughty boy. 'Wolf.'

TRISH What? Where is he?

FRANK 'Wolf — wolf.'

BERNA He's not there at all?

FRANK 'Fraid not. Woke you up all the same, didn't it?

TERRY (*Quiet fury*) That is not funny, for Christ's sake.

TRISH Oh, Frank, how could you?

FRANK Joke.

ANGELA (*Calmly*) Damn you, Frank.

FRANK A joke — that's all.

TERRY Not funny at all, Frank.

FRANK Sorry.

TRISH Oh, Frank, that was cruel.

FRANK Sorry — sorry — sorry. For God's sake what's eating you all?

> *Again they retreat into themselves. And as they do*
> GEORGE *plays 'Regina caeli, laetari, alleluia; quia quem*
> *meruisti portare — ' He breaks off mid-phrase. Silence.*

ANGELA (*Suddenly, with great energy*) Alright, everybody! Story-time! So we're stuck here! We're going nowhere! We'll pass the night with stories.

TRISH Good for you, Angela. Yeah-yeah-yeah-yeah!

ANGELA 'Once upon a time — ' Who goes first? Terry!

TERRY I don't know any stories.

TRISH Yes, you do. He's a wonderful story-teller.

ANGELA We'll get him later. You start off, Trish.

TRISH Let someone else start. I'll go second. Berna, tell us one of your law stories.

BERNA Alright. Let me think of one.

TRISH A clean law story! We'll come back to you. Frank — 'Once upon a time.'

FRANK Pass.

TERRY Get it over with, Frank.

TRISH Come on, Frank. Be a sport. It's only a bit of fun.

FRANK Later. After Berna.

ANGELA I think George wants to go first.

FRANK What about yourself, Terry?

TERRY Couldn't tell a story to save my life.

ANGELA Have you a story to tell, George?

TRISH What's wrong with you all? You go first, Angela. Then a clean law story. Then Frank. Then —

ANGELA George?

GEORGE Yes?

TRISH Then me. Then Terry —

ANGELA George will go first. Tell us your story, George.

TRISH Right — I'll kick off.

ANGELA (*To* GEORGE) 'Once upon a time — '

FRANK Stop bullying, Angela.

GEORGE *moves into the centre of the group.*

TRISH This woman had ten children, one after the other, and —

ANGELA Right, George?

TERRY Angela —

ANGELA (*To* GEORGE) Ready?

TRISH And the ten children all had red hair like the —

ANGELA (*To* TRISH) Please. (*To* GEORGE) 'Once upon a time — '

Silence. GEORGE *looks at each of them in turn. Then he plays the first fifteen seconds of the Third Movement (Presto) of Beethoven's Sonata No. 14 (Moonlight). He plays with astonishing virtuosity, very rapidly, much faster than the piece is scored, and with an internal fury; so that his performance, as well as being dazzlingly dexterous and skillful and fast — because of its dazzling dexterity and skill and speed — seems close to parody. And then in the middle of a phrase, he suddenly stops. He bows to them all very formally, as if he had given a recital in a concert hall.*

GEORGE Thank you. Thank you very much.

He now removes the accordion and puts it in the case.
Pause.

TRISH (*Almost shouting, very emotional, close to tears*) Are you
satisfied now? Happy now, are you? Do you see you
all? Not one of you is fit to clean his boots!

GEORGE *now spreads out a sleeping-bag and lies on top
of it.* TRISH *spreads a rug over him. Pause.*

BERNA I'm going for a swim. Anybody coming?
TERRY Please, Berna; not now.
BERNA Angela?
TERRY That water could be dangerous, Berna.
ANGELA Wait until daybreak. I'll go with you then. I'd love a
swim, too. As soon as it's daylight.

FRANK *comes down from the cat-walk. He goes to*
TERRY.

FRANK Waiting — just waiting — waiting for anything makes
you a bit edgy, doesn't it? Sorry about that 'wolf' thing.

TERRY *makes a gesture of dismissal and continues
looking through the hampers.*

It wasn't meant cruelly. Just stupid.
TERRY Brandied Peaches and Romanian Truffles. Christ. I
order two hampers of good food and they fill them
with stuff nobody can eat. (*He holds up a bottle*) Drop of
brandy?
FRANK If you had some whiskey.
TERRY Should have.
FRANK Can't take it neat though.
TERRY (*Searching hamper*) Of course — everything except
water.

*He points to a shallow hollow on the floor of the pier
where water has gathered.*

Is that rain-water or salt-water?

FRANK *dips a finger and tastes it.*

FRANK We're in business.

FRANK *scoops some water into a paper cup and makes a drink.*

(*Toasts*) Happy birthday, Terry.

TERRY That was yesterday.

FRANK Was it? All the same.

TERRY How's the book coming on?

FRANK The finishing post is in sight ... at last. Time for it, says you, after three-and-a-half years.

TERRY Great.

FRANK I know I shouldn't say this but I hope — Goddamn it, I pray — this is going to be the breakthrough for me. And some instinct tells me it will. Well ... maybe ... touch wood.

TERRY You've told me a dozen times — I'm sorry — clock-making through the ages — is that it?

FRANK Terence!

TERRY Sorry.

FRANK *The Measurement of Time and Its Effect on European Civilisation.*

TERRY Ah.

FRANK I know. But they assure me there is a market for it — not large but world-wide. It *is* fascinating stuff. I never seem to thank you for all your help, Terry.

TERRY Nothing — nothing. Another splash?

He pours more whiskey into the cup.

FRANK How can I thank you adequately? Only for you I'd still be sitting in that estate-agent's office. Instead of which — ta-ra! — the thrilling life of a journeyman writer, scrounging commissions. Angela going back to lecturing after all these years — that was a huge help, too, of course. And the poor girl hates it, hates it. But your

support, Terry, every bloody week — magnanimous! I
hope some day I'll —

TERRY Don't talk about it. Please.

FRANK A new Medici.

TERRY Is that a horse?

FRANK You know very well —

TERRY I'd put money on that myself!

FRANK Thanks. That's all I can say. Thank you.

He finishes his drink rapidly and makes another. TRISH
puts a pillow under GEORGE's *head.*

TRISH Lift your head. Good. Are you warm enough? That's
better.

FRANK I annoyed Trish a while ago. She said I was cheap,
joking about apparitions out there.

TERRY She has her hands full.

FRANK Tough life. Courageous lady.

TERRY Yes. So — the clock book — when is it going to appear?

FRANK Another apparition. This time next year, we hope.
Actually I was thinking of doing a chapter on apparitions — well, visions, hallucinations, whatever.

TERRY In a book about clocks?

FRANK Time measurement, Terry! Did you know that the
accurate measurement of time changed monastic
practices in the Middle Ages, when Saint Conall and
company flourished out there? See? You never knew
that! Before that, monks prayed a few times during the
day — a casual discipline that depended on nature —
maybe at cock-crow, at high noon, when it got too dark
to work in the fields. But Saint Benedict wanted more
than that from his monks: he wanted continuous
prayer. And with the invention of clocks that became
possible.

TERRY But there weren't clocks then, were there?

FRANK No, no; crude time-pieces; sophisticated egg-timers.
But with these new instruments you could break the
twenty-four hours into exact sections. And once you
could do that, once you could waken your monks up at
fixed hours two or three times a night, suddenly — (*He*

claps his hands) — continuous prayer!

TERRY What has that to do with apparitions?

FRANK Think about it. At the stroke of midnight — at 2.00 a.m. — at 4.00 a.m. — at 6.00 a.m. you chase your monks out of their warm beds. Into a freezing chapel. Fasting. Deprived of sleep. Repeating the same chant over and over again. And because they're hungry and disoriented and giddy for want of sleep and repeating the same droning chant over and over again, of course they hallucinate — see apparitions — whatever. Wouldn't you?

TERRY (*Laughs*) Frank!

FRANK Honestly! Medieval monks were always seeing apparitions. Read their books. And all because of the invention of time-pieces. A word of warning, Terry. Be careful at matins — that's just before dawn. That's when you're most susceptible.

TERRY Is that going to be in your book!

FRANK Maybe. Why not? Anything to explain away the wonderful, the mystery.

TERRY But you don't believe a word of that, do you?

FRANK How would I know? But there must be some explanation, mustn't there? The mystery offends — so the mystery has to be extracted. (*He points to the island*) They had their own way of dealing with it: they embraced it all — everything. Yes, yes, yes, they said; why bloody not? A rage for the absolute, Terry — that's what they had. And because their acceptance was so comprehensive, so open, so generous, maybe they *were* put in touch — what do you think? — so intimately in touch that maybe, maybe they actually *did* see.

TERRY In touch with what? See what?

FRANK Whatever it is we desire but can't express. What is beyond language. The inexpressible. The ineffable.

TERRY To spend their lives out there in the Atlantic, I suppose they must have been on to something.

FRANK And even if they were in touch, even if they actually did see, they couldn't have told us, could they, unless they had the speech of angels? Because there is no vocabulary for the experience. Because language stands baffled before all that and says of what it has attempted to say, 'No, no! That's not it at all! No, not at all!' (*He drinks rapidly*) Or maybe they did write it all down — without benefit of words! That's the only way it could be written, isn't it? A book without words!

TERRY You've lost me, Frank.

FRANK And if they accomplished that, they'd have written the last book ever written — and the most wonderful! And then, Terry, then maybe life would cease!

He laughs. Brief pause.

Or maybe we've got it all wrong as usual, Terry. Maybe Saint Conall stood on the shores of the island there and gazed across here at Ballybeg and said to his monks, 'Oh, lads, lads, *there* is the end of desire. Whoever lives there lives at the still core of it all. Happy, happy, lucky people'. What do you think?

FRANK *is now very animated. He laughs again. He drinks again.*

TERRY That's us — happy people.

FRANK (*Calls*) Come and join us, Conall! It's all in place here! (*To* TERRY) Well — why not?

TERRY Indeed.

FRANK (*Laughs*) Despite appearances.

TERRY Why not?

TERRY *fills the outstretched cup again.*

FRANK Can't drink it without water.

TERRY Any left in the holy well?

FRANK Enough.

Again he scoops up water and makes a drink.

Aren't you joining me?

TERRY Pass this time. To the book.

FRANK No, no, not to the book. The book's nothing, nothing at all; a silly game of blind-man's buff. No, to the other, to the mystery itself, Terry. To the goddamn wonderful, maddening, necessary mystery.

He shudders as if with cold.

TERRY You're cold in that shirt. Here. Put this on.

TERRY *takes off his jacket and puts it round* FRANK's *shoulders.*

That's definitely your colour.

FRANK And to my goddamn wonderful wife. Is it profane to talk about her in the same breath as the sacred?

TERRY Is it?

FRANK Look at her. Now there's an apparition. She's . . . miraculous in that light, isn't she? Fourteen years married and the blood still thunders in my head when I look at her . . . . Have you any idea, Terry, have you any idea at all of the turmoil, the panic people like me live in — the journeymen, the clerks of the world? No, no, the goddamn failures, for Christ's sake.

TERRY Frank, you —

FRANK Of course I am. Husband — father — provider — worthless.

TERRY Your book will —

FRANK The great book! (*He makes a huge gesture of dismissal*) She pretends to believe in it, too. But she's such a bright woman — she knows, she knows. You both know. Oh Jesus, Terry, if only you knew, have you any idea at all just how fragile it all is . . . ? (*Calls*) Maybe you should stay where you are, lads. It's not quite all in place here yet . . . . Damn good whiskey. What is it? Coleraine 1922! That's very special. May I help myself? (*Proclaims*) Lord, it *is* good for us to be here! Isn't it . . . ?

He moves away. Pause.

ANGELA (*Softly, tentatively*) Oh my God . . .

TERRY   What is it?

ANGELA   Oh God, is it . . . ?

TRISH   What's the matter, Angela?

ANGELA   I think — oh God — I think —

TRISH   Angela, are you sick?

ANGELA   There's our boat.

BERNA   Where?

TRISH   Stop that, Angela.

FRANK   Where? Where is it?

GEORGE *sits up*.

BERNA   I see no boat.

TERRY   Where is it, Angela?

FRANK   Are you sure?

TRISH   Where? — Show me — where? (*To* GEORGE) The boat's here, she says.

ANGELA   (*Points*) There. It is, Terry, isn't it?

TRISH   Is it, Terry?

BERNA   There is no boat.

ANGELA   Oh God, Terry, that's our boat — isn't it?

TRISH   Point to it.

ANGELA   Maybe it's only — can you see nothing? — That patch of light on the water — just beyond that I thought I saw —

FRANK   Nothing. There's nothing.

TRISH   Where's the patch of light?

BERNA   There's no patch of light.

TERRY   Is it anywhere near that mist?

FRANK   Nothing. All in her head.

ANGELA   He's right . . . sorry . . . nothing . . . for a minute I was certain . . . sorry . . .

BERNA   You shouldn't do that, Angela.

ANGELA   Sorry.

BERNA   You really shouldn't do that.

ANGELA   I'm very sorry. I really am.

TERRY   There *is* a patch of light there; if you stare at it long enough it seems to make shapes . . . . Anyhow, no harm done.

Pause.

(*Privately to* ANGELA) I ordered your favourite chocolate mints. Somebody must have eaten them. I suspect Charlie.

ANGELA The boatman?

TERRY My driver. Minibus Charlie. How could you forget Charlie? And the boatman's name is Carlin.

ANGELA Give me a drink, Terry, would you?

TERRY Wine? — Gin? — Vodka?

ANGELA Anything at all. Just a drop.

BERNA *suddenly stands up and proclaims:*

BERNA Alright! I'll tell my story now!

TRISH Good girl, Berna.

BERNA I had a different psychiatrist in the clinic last week, a very intense young Englishman called Walsingham. He told me this story.

ANGELA (*Accepting drink from* TERRY) Thanks.

TERRY Anybody else?

FRANK Quiet.

TRISH Attention, please. (*To* BERNA) 'Once upon a time . . . '

BERNA Not once upon a time, Trish. I can give you the exact date: 1294. And in the year 1294, in the village of Nazareth, in the land that is now called Israel, a very wonderful thing happened. There was in the village a small, white-washed house built of rough stone, just like these; and for over a thousand years the villagers looked on that house as their most wonderful possession; because that house had been the home of Mary and Joseph and their baby, Jesus.

And then in the year 1294, on the seventh day of March, an amazing thing happened. That small, white-washed house rose straight up into the air, right away up into the sky. It hung there for a few seconds as if it was a bird finding its bearings. Then it floated — flew — over the Mediterranean Sea, high up over the Island of Crete, across the Aegean Sea, until it came to the coast of Italy. It crossed that coast and came to a stop

directly above a small town called Loreto in the centre
of Italy. Then it began to descend, slowly down and
down and down, until it came to rest in the centre of
the town. And there it sits to this day. And it is known
as the Holy House of Loreto — a place of pilgrimage,
revered and attested to by hundreds of thousands of
pilgrims every year. The Holy House of Loreto.

Nobody knows how to respond. Pause.

TRISH   A flying house? . . . And it's there now? . . . Well,
heavens above, isn't that a —
BERNA   And because it took off and flew across the sea and
landed safely again, all over the world Our Lady of
Loreto is known as the Patron Saint of Aviation.

Another brief pause.

FRANK   There you are . . .
TRISH   (*Breezily*) Good girl, Berna.
FRANK   Never knew that . . .
TRISH   Live and learn.
FRANK   Indeed . . . live and learn . . .
TERRY   Wonderful story, Berna. Well done.
FRANK   Terry says this is my colour. What do you think?
BERNA   In our second year we had a lecturer in Equity, a
Scotsman called — I've forgotten his name. We called
him Offence to Reason because he used that phrase in
every single lecture. We used to wait for it to come.
'Does that constitute an offence to reason?' (*Laughs*) He
was in awe of reason. He really believed reason was
the key to 'truth', the 'big verities'.
TERRY   The sun's trying to come up, is it?
BERNA   No, it's not a wonderful story, Trish. It's a stupid story.
And crude. And pig-headed. A flying house is an
offence to reason, isn't it? It marches up to reason and
belts it across the gob and says to it, 'Fuck you,
reason. I'm as good as you any day. You haven't all the
fucking answers — not by any means'. That's what
Dr Walsingham's story says. And that's why I like it.

She begins to cry quietly. TERRY *moves towards her. But*
TRISH *holds up her hand and he stops. Then* TRISH *goes*
to her and holds her.

TRISH Shhh, love, shhh . . .
BERNA (*Into* TRISH's *face*) It's defiance, Trish — that's what I
like about it.
TRISH I know . . . I know . . .
BERNA It's stupid, futile defiance.
TRISH Shhh . . .

She moves away from TRISH *and goes to the end of the*
pier. Her narrative has charged the atmosphere with
unease, with anxiety.

FRANK (*Breezily*) You're right, Terry; the sun is trying to come
up.
TERRY Yes?

FRANK *begins singing the chorus of 'The World is*
Waiting for the Sunrise'. TERRY *joins him. They sing*
two lines.

FRANK You and I could do a neat dance to that, Berna. George?

GEORGE *does not play.*

TRISH George is tired. He (*Frank*) knows the words of every-
thing. What sort of a head have you got?
FRANK (*Brightly*) Full of rubbish. And panic.
ANGELA Did you bring a swim-suit, Berna?

No answer. BERNA *now moves up to the cat-walk.*

TRISH (*To* BERNA) I brought mine. You can have mine.
FRANK Or better still, Berna — I say, I say, I say — you may
have mine!
ANGELA We're all too tired, Frank.
FRANK Are we?

He sings the first two lines of the refrain of 'Lazy River'.
Brief pause.

Right, Trish — all set?

TRISH What?

FRANK You're next!

TRISH What's he talking about?

FRANK For a story!

TERRY Yes, Trish!

TRISH I don't know any —

TERRY You're a wonderful story-teller. Isn't she, Berna?

TRISH Ah, come on, Terry. You know very well —

ANGELA Go on, Trish!

FRANK Any kind of fiction will do us.

ANGELA Myth — fantasy —

TERRY A funny story —

ANGELA A good lie —

FRANK Even a bad lie. Look at us for God's sake — we'll accept anything! Right, Berna?

Now TRISH *understands that their purpose is to engage* BERNA *again.*

TRISH You want a story? Right!

She jumps to her feet and launches into her performance with great theatricality and brio.

So I'm on then? Alright-alright-alright!

FRANK Certainly are.

TRISH (*Stalling, improvising*) You want a story?

ANGELA We need a story.

TERRY Come down and hear this, Berna.

BERNA *looks over the wall.*

TRISH A story. Absolutely. Yes. Once upon a time and a very long time ago —

TERRY She's bluffing.

ANGELA Terry!

TERRY Look at her eyes.

FRANK What do her eyes say, George?

ANGELA (*To* TRISH) Pay no attention to him (*Terry*). Once upon a time . . . ?

TRISH May I proceed?

FRANK Let the lady speak.

TERRY That's no lady — that-sa ma sista.

ANGELA Terry!

TRISH Once upon a time and a very long time ago —

FRANK *sings the first line of 'Just a Song at Twilight'.*

ANGELA Please, Frank.

Suddenly TRISH *knows what her story is.*

TRISH The morning we got married, George! Okay?

GEORGE Okay.

FRANK Good one. Yeah.

ANGELA What story's that?

TRISH May I, George?

GEORGE Go ahead.

ANGELA I've forgotten that story.

TERRY That's a boring story, Trish.

FRANK Is it? Great! Boring is soothing.

ANGELA Do I know the story?

FRANK Boring reassures.

TERRY Course you do.

FRANK I'm all for boring. Sedate us, Trish.

TRISH If I may continue . . . ?

FRANK And it came to pass —

TRISH Twenty-two years ago. St Theresa's church.

FRANK Parish of Drumragh.

TRISH Ten o'clock Mass.

TERRY Best man. (*He bows*)

TRISH And little Patricia, all a-quiver in gold tiara, cream chiffon dress and pale blue shoes with three-quarter heels, has left her home for the last time and —

FRANK (*Sings*) 'There was I — ' George?

GEORGE *picks up his accordion.*

TERRY   You were bridesmaid, Berna. Remember?

ANGELA   (*Remembering*) It's the story of the missing — !

FRANK   Don't! (*Interrupt*)

TRISH   May I? She arrives at the door of St Theresa's. And now her little heart starts to flutter because just as she enters the church on her Daddy's arm, Miss Quirk begins to play the harmonium —

> *She is suddenly drowned out by* GEORGE *playing the first line of 'There was I' — which is immediately picked up by* FRANK.

FRANK   (*Sings*) ' — waiting at the church — ' That's it! 'Waiting at the church — ' Terry!

> TERRY *and* FRANK *do a dance/march routine and sing together:*

DUET   'Waiting at the church / When I found — '

FRANK   What?

TERRY   ' — he'd left me in the lurch — ' Angela!

ANGELA   (*Sings*) 'Oh how it did upset me — '

> TERRY *and* FRANK *sing 'Tra-la-la-la-la'.*

Sorry, Trish.

TRISH   (*Pretended anger*) Fine — fine —

ANGELA   Behave yourselves, you two!

TRISH   Have your own fun.

FRANK   Please, Trish —

TRISH   No point, is there?

FRANK   Go on, Patricia. 'The flutter bride was all a-chiffon — '

TRISH   See?

TERRY   Anyhow we all know how the story ends, don't we?

FRANK   So what? All we want of a story is to hear it again and again and again and again and again.

ANGELA   Are you going to let the girl finish?

FRANK   And so it came to pass . . .

GEORGE *now plays Wagner's 'Wedding March' very softly, with a reverence close to mockery.*

TRISH Thank you, George. (*She blows him a kiss*) The church is full to overflowing. My modest eyes are still on the ground. Daddy's gaze is manfully direct. We walk up that aisle together with quiet dignity until we come to the altar —

FRANK She's a natural!

TRISH And then for the first time I raise those modest eyes so that I can feast them on my handsome groom-to-be, my beloved George.

FRANK Yes?

TRISH But lo —

FRANK Go on!

TRISH Who steps out to receive me — ?

FRANK But —

TERRY The anxious bookie — the groomsman!

FRANK Groomsman? Where's the groom?

TRISH No groom. No George.

Howls of dismay.

ANGELA Shame, George, shame!

FRANK Where can he be?

TERRY (*Calls*) George!

FRANK (*Calls*) We need you, George!

TERRY (*Calls*) Where are you, George?

FRANK (*Calls*) Heeelp!

FRANK ⎫
TERRY ⎭ (*Call*) Heeelp!

ANGELA Will you let the girl finish her story?

TRISH Haven't seen him for over a week. Last heard from him two days ago from Limerick —

TERRY Cork.

TRISH — where the Aeolians — Michael Robinson and himself — they've been giving Beethoven recitals in schools and colleges there.

TERRY Knew she'd get it wrong.

FRANK (*To* TERRY) Please.

TRISH But these concerts, I know, are finished. Why isn't he here?

TERRY Playing with the Dude Ranchers.

TRISH Why isn't he here for his wedding?

TERRY Finishing a tour in County Cork.

TRISH Terry, the Aeolians were in Limerick doing a series of —

TERRY The Aeolians had broken up three months before you got married.

TRISH Don't you think I might — ?

TERRY George was working full-time with the Ranchers when you and he got married.

TRISH Terry —

FRANK Those details don't —

TERRY That's why George packed in the Aeolians — to make some money — so that you and he could get married. Right, George?

ANGELA So what? The point of Trish's story is —

TERRY (*To* TRISH) You asked me to take George on. Don't you remember?

TRISH So that when we — ?

TERRY And that's when the Ranchers really took off. When he packed in the Aeolians and joined the Ranchers. He made the Ranchers. We would never have come to anything without George.

TRISH *is totally bewildered.*

TRISH But how could I? . . . God . . . And when did — ?

TERRY You've forgotten — that's all. (*He hugs her quickly*) I'd signed George up three months before your wedding.

ANGELA And all this has nothing to do with the story. The point is that he did turn up at St Theresa's — and only ten minutes late. Well done, George.

TERRY (*To* TRISH) I didn't mean to —

TRISH But how could I have — ?

FRANK Certainly did turn up. On a motorbike — right? Soaked through and purple with cold.

ANGELA With the wedding-suit in a rucksack on his back.

FRANK Changed in the organ-loft — remember?

TRISH Oh my God, how could that have happened?

ANGELA That was a good day.

FRANK Great day.

TERRY (*To* TRISH) Sorry.

FRANK A wonderful day . . . God . . . what a day that was . . .

ANGELA Well done, Trish. A great story. The best story yet. Very well done.

> *Silence. Again they withdraw into themselves.* BERNA *now climbs from the cat-walk up to the top wall. As she does she hums 'O, Mother, I Could Weep'. She walks along the top of the wall.* TERRY *now sees her.*

TERRY Berna, please come down from there.

FRANK Berna!

TERRY That is dangerous, Berna.

TRISH (*To* TERRY) For God's sake bring her down!

ANGELA Berna, love —

TERRY (*Command*) Come down, Berna! At once!

> BERNA, *still humming, is now at the end of the wall. Without looking at anybody she jumps into the sea.*

FRANK Berna!

TERRY Jesus!

ANGELA Berna!

TERRY Oh Jesus Christ . . . !

> *End of Act One.*

ACT TWO

Before the lights go up we hear GEORGE *playing 'All things bright and beautiful, all creatures great and small, / All things wise and wonderful, the Lord God made them all'.*

At that point lights up. A new day has opened. A high sky. A pristine and brilliant morning sunlight that enfolds the pier like an aureole and renovates everything it touches.

BERNA, *a cardigan round her shoulders, is in different clothes — her Act One clothes are drying across a bollard.* TRISH *is brushing and combing* BERNA's *hair.* TERRY *is up on the cat-walk, looking casually across the landscape, occasionally using binoculars.* ANGELA *is playing a game she has invented. From a distance of about five feet she pitches stones (lobster-pot weights) at an empty bottle placed close to the life-belt stand. (When the game ends there is a small mound of stones.) On the life-belt stand now hangs — as well as Angela's sun hat from Act One — the silk scarf Berna wore in Act One.* GEORGE *continues playing: 'Each little flower that opens, each little bird that sings, / He made their glowing colours, he made their tiny wings. / All things bright and beautiful, all creatures great and small — '*

Now ANGELA *sings to the music:*

ANGELA 'All things wise and wonderful, the Lord God makes them all.' You are 'wise and wonderful', George: you're the only one of us that slept all night.

GEORGE Did I?

ANGELA For an hour. And you snore.

GEORGE Sorry. (*He beckons her to him*) If I ever decide to go, I want your children to have this (*accordion*).

ANGELA You are going —

GEORGE One of them might take it up.

ANGELA George, that's —

GEORGE Bit battered but it's working alright.

ANGELA That's a lovely thought. (*She kisses him*) Thank you.

GEORGE *If* I ever decide to go.

65

TERRY Where did Frank say he was going?

ANGELA To take photographs, he said. Probably to beat the head off poor old Carlin.

Pause.

TERRY Listen to those birds.

ANGELA Larks, are they?

TERRY 'And they heard the song of coloured birds.' You wouldn't believe me.

ANGELA They're larks, Terry. Ordinary larks.

GEORGE *begins to play 'Skylark' very softly.*

Exactly, George.

TERRY Has it a name, that game?

ANGELA It's called: how close can you get without touching it. Anybody got the time?

TERRY Just after seven.

BERNA (*Looks at her watch*) Stopped. Salt-water finished it.

ANGELA When does the minibus come for us?

TERRY Half-an-hour or so.

BERNA *takes off her watch, shakes it and holds it to her ear.*

BERNA That's that.

She casually tosses it into the sea. Only TRISH *sees this.*

TERRY There must be hundreds of them (*birds*). And they *are* coloured.

TRISH (*Quietly*) You put the heart across us, Berna, jumping into the sea like that.

BERNA Are you nearly finished? (*Hair-dressing*)

TRISH You shouldn't have done that.

BERNA I wanted a swim.

TRISH It was a naughty thing to do. It was a cruel thing to do.

BERNA I told you — I wanted a swim.

TRISH Particularly cruel to Terry.

BERNA Oh poor Terry. (*She stands up abruptly*) That's fine, Trish. Thank you. (*To* ANGELA) May I play?

ANGELA Of course.

TERRY Well, would you look at that! Carlin has lit his fire again! (*Laughs*) What a strange man.

ANGELA (*To* BERNA) There are stones over there.

TERRY Maybe he'll come for us after he's had his breakfast. What do you think?

TRISH (*Wearily*) Terry.

ANGELA (*To* TRISH) Going to play?

TRISH Yes.

TERRY We still have time for a quick dart out and straight back. We'd do it in less than an hour.

TRISH D'you know what I would love? A cup of strong tea!

TERRY There's still a chance. Why not? I'm offering five-to-one against. Three-to-one. Any takers?

> GEORGE *has come to the last line of 'Skylark'.* TRISH *sings the line. The music stops.*

TRISH Now tell us what to do.

ANGELA The aim is to get as close as possible to that bottle. But every time you touch it you lose a point.

TRISH You *lose* a point? What sort of a makey-up game is that!

TERRY Looks wonderful in this light (*the island*). I'm not giving up. Two-to-one against. Even money.

TRISH We should all be exhausted, shouldn't we? But I feel . . . exhilarated. Play something exhilarating, George.

> GEORGE *plays 'Regina Caeli' right through. Immediately he begins:*

That's not exhilarating, is it?

ANGELA (*To* TRISH) Your throw.

BERNA Is there a chill in the air?

TRISH (*Preparing to throw*) Right.

> BERNA *reaches out to take her scarf from the life-belt stand.*

ANGELA *(Quickly)* No; take mine. It's warmer. Like a hall-stand, isn't it? Good one, Trish. You have the hang of it.

> BERNA *drapes Angela's scarf around her shoulders.* FRANK *enters.*

FRANK Well — well — well! What Eden is this? And what happy people have we here, besporting themselves in the sunlight?

TERRY *(Coming down)* We thought we had lost you.

FRANK For you, George. Found it in the sand-dunes back there.

> *Music stops.*

GEORGE Yes?

FRANK Interesting, isn't it? Polished flint-stone. The head of an axe, I think.

GEORGE Thank you.

FRANK That's the hole for the handle. Beautifully shaped, isn't it?

GEORGE Lovely.

TERRY Where did you find it?

FRANK Just behind the pier. Probably buried in the sand at one time. Then the sand shifted.

TERRY May I see it?

GEORGE Thank you, Frank.

FRANK Some weapon. That's a lethal edge there.

TERRY And the weight of it.

FRANK We'll make a handle for it; and on your next tour, if audiences aren't appreciative enough —

> *He mimes striking with the axe.*

TERRY That *is* sharp.

FRANK Meant for business, that weapon.

TERRY Did you get some good pictures?

FRANK Don't talk to me about pictures! Tell you all in a moment.

> *He goes to* BERNA *and presents her with a bunch of wild flowers.*

68

For you, my lady. (*He kisses her*)

BERNA Oh, Frank.

ANGELA Aren't they pretty? Look at that blue.

TRISH You got them around here?

FRANK Just over the sand-dunes.

TRISH (*To* GEORGE) He's a *real* gentleman.

FRANK (*To* BERNA) And d'you know what? — I could eat you in that dress.

BERNA They're beautiful, Frank. Thank you.

FRANK Welcome.

ANGELA Now — Berna. (*The game*)

TRISH You want to know how it's really done, girls? Just watch this.

They continue playing.

TERRY Lovely flowers. Thank you.

FRANK The place is full of them.

TERRY We thought maybe you'd gone to chastise Mr Carlin.

FRANK Just before daybreak there was a white mist suspended above the island; like a white silk canopy. And as the sun got up you could see the mist dissolve and vanish. So of course I thought: Oileán Draíochta emerging from behind its veil — capture this for posterity!

TERRY Did you get it?

FRANK Two bloody spools of it. Wasted all my film.

ANGELA (*To* TRISH) Not bad. Not bad.

TRISH Not bad? Wonderful!

BERNA Very close, Trish. Good one.

TRISH I think this could well be my game. Want to play, Frank?

FRANK (*To* ALL) Listen to this. You won't believe what I saw out there, Trish.

TRISH What?

Brief pause.

BERNA What did you see, Frank?

FRANK *looks at them. He is not sure if he will tell his story.*

FRANK Just as the last wisp of the veil was melting away, suddenly — as if it had been waiting for a sign — suddenly a dolphin rose up out of the sea. And for thirty seconds, maybe a minute, it danced for me. Like a faun, a satyr; with its manic, leering face. Danced with a deliberate, controlled, exquisite abandon. Leaping, twisting, tumbling, gyrating in wild and intricate contortions. And for that thirty seconds, maybe a minute, I could swear it never once touched the water — was free of it — had nothing to do with water. A performance — that's what it was. A performance so considered, so aware, that you knew it knew it was being witnessed, wanted to be witnessed. Thrilling; and wonderful; and at the same time — I don't know why — at the same time . . . with that manic, leering face . . . somehow very disturbing.

BERNA Did you get pictures of it?

FRANK Nothing. You'd almost think it waited until my last shot was used up before it appeared. Thirty seconds, maybe a minute . . . Unbelievable. (*Embarrassed laugh*) Another apparition, Terry.

TERRY Maybe.

Pause. FRANK *is now embarrassed at his own intensity and because the others are all staring at him. He laughs again.*

FRANK So I saw a porpoise or a dolphin or something leap out of the water and dance about a bit. Wonderful!

TRISH I love dolphins. I think they are terrific. (*Briskly*) Right. Who's next?

ANGELA, TRISH *and* BERNA *play their game.*

FRANK Left them speechless, didn't it? My Ballybeg epiphany.

TERRY Sorry I missed that.

FRANK (*To* GEORGE) Upset me, that damn thing, for some reason.

GEORGE *nods and smiles.*

TERRY Drink?

FRANK (*Gestures: No*) Could have done with one back there. It really was a ceremonial dance, Terry — honest to God. And they look so damned knowing — don't they? — with those almost human faces . . . . I'm getting to like this (*jacket*).

TERRY Well, what are our chances?

FRANK Chances?

> TERRY *indicates Carlin's house.*

Forget him. Next time we'll bring our own boat.

TERRY Sorry. Not allowed.

FRANK Maybe you're right. Maybe he still will come. Who's to say?

> TERRY *moves to the end of the pier where he sits by himself.*

ANGELA That hit the bottle. Point lost, Trish.

TRISH Didn't hit it, did it?

ANGELA Sorry. Point down. Berna?

> BERNA, *her flowers still in her hand, picks up a stone close to* FRANK. *At the same time she puts one of her flowers in her hair and blows a kiss to him. As she does this* GEORGE *plays 'Bring Flowers of the Rarest'.*

GEORGE 'Bring flowers of the rarest, bring blossoms the fairest
From garden and woodland and hillside and dale,
Our full hearts are swelling, our glad voices telling
The praise of the loveliest flower of the vale.'

> *Immediately after he plays the first line — 'Bring flowers . . . fairest' and as he continues playing:*

TRISH I know that song, don't I?

FRANK So do I.

BERNA It's a hymn — is it?

GEORGE Guess.

FRANK It *is* a hymn — isn't it?

BERNA Play the chorus, George.

TRISH I do know it, whatever it is.

FRANK I do, too.

> GEORGE *now begins the chorus, 'O Mary we crown thee with blossoms today — '*

TRISH Yes! (*Sings*) ' — Queen of the angels and queen of the May — '

FRANK Haven't heard that since I was a child.

TRISH ⎫ (*Sing*) 'O Mary we crown thee with blossoms today,
BERNA ⎭   Queen of the angels and queen of the May.'

BERNA (*To* GEORGE) Thank you.

FRANK Not since I was a child.

> *Brief pause. And immediately* ANGELA *plunges into 'Oh Dem Golden Slippers'. And as she sings* GEORGE *accompanies her. She picks up Frank's shoes, and singing loudly, raucously, defiantly, and waving the shoes above her head, she parades/dances around the pier. She sings the entire chorus. She stops suddenly. The performance is over.*
>
> *Pause. Now she sings very softly the first two lines of the chorus of 'I Don't Know Why I'm Happy'. She tails off listlessly. She looks at the shoes and tosses them over to where* FRANK *is sitting. She looks at them all.*

ANGELA What a goddamn, useless, endless, unhappy outing this has been! (*Pause*) I'm sorry, Terry . . .

> *Pause.*

FRANK (*To* TERRY) May I? (*Drink*)

> FRANK *pours a drink and scoops up water.*

Should do a rain-dance. Well's almost dry.

> TERRY *now rises and joins them.*

TERRY I just remembered — I do have a story.

TRISH Too late, Terry. Story-time's over.

FRANK No, it's not. It's always story-time. Right, Berna?

BERNA Is it?

FRANK Certainly is.

TRISH Alright. But make it short, Terry. Short and funny. I need a laugh.

FRANK Terence . . . ?

TERRY Yes. Well. The solicitor who is handling the sale of Oileán Draíochta — he told me this story. We were having lunch together. No; we had finished eating. He was having coffee and I was having tea and we both —

TRISH The story, Terry.

TERRY (*Almost reluctantly*) Yes — yes — the story. Well, the story he told me was this. Many years ago a young man was killed out there.

BERNA Killed how?

TERRY I suppose . . . murdered.

FRANK God.

TERRY His name was Sean O'Boyle. He was seventeen years of age. If you were to believe my solicitor friend he was . . . ritually killed.

TRISH What do you mean?

TERRY A group of young people — he was one of them — seven young men and seven young women. It wasn't a disagreement, a fight; nothing like that. They were all close friends.

ANGELA And what happened?

TERRY The evidence suggests some sort of ritual, during which young O'Boyle was . . . (*He shrugs*)

TRISH Oh my God.

BERNA What evidence?

TERRY Burned out fires — empty wine bottles — clothes left behind — blood smeared on rocks. It's thought there was some sort of orgy. Anyhow at some point they dismembered him. That's accurate enough — from the pieces they found.

FRANK Jesus Christ, Terry . . . Oh Jesus Christ . . .

ANGELA When did this happen?

TERRY 1932. On the night of June 26.

ANGELA These young people — they were from here?

TERRY Part of a group from this parish who had just returned from Dublin from the Eucharistic Congress. The older people went straight to their homes. The young group — our fourteen — apparently they had been drinking all the way home from Dublin — they stole a half-decker — from this pier actually — and headed out for Oileán Draíochta. Some people say they had *poitín* stashed out there and that one of the girls was a great fiddler and that they just went out to have a dance. My friend has his own theory. These people were peasants, from a very remote part of the country. And he believes they were still in a state of intoxication after the Congress — it was the most spectacular, the most incredible thing they had ever witnessed. And that ferment and the wine and the music and the dancing . . .

TRISH I don't know what you're saying, Terry.

TERRY That young O'Boyle was . . . sacrificed.

FRANK Jesus Christ.

BERNA The other thirteen — they were charged?

TERRY No charges were ever brought.

TRISH Why not?

ANGELA The police weren't brought in?

TERRY Oh, yes. But by then the situation was away beyond their control. The parish was in uproar. Passions were at boiling point. Families were physically attacking one another. The police were helpless. The only person who could control the situation was the bishop of the time. He had led the group that had just made the pilgrimage to the Eucharistic Congress. And every year on August 15 he organised a pilgrimage out to the island.

TRISH So?

TERRY So the thirteen were summoned to the bishop's palace. All that is known is that they made a solemn pledge never to divulge what happened that night on the island; that they had to leave the country immediately and forever; and that before the end of the week they had all left for Australia.

TRISH Oh my God.

BERNA So nobody was ever charged?

TERRY Nobody. O'Boyle was an only child. Both his parents were dead within the year.

ANGELA Oileán Draíochta — wonderful.

TERRY Then the war came. Times were bad. People moved away. Within ten years the area was depopulated — that's your derelict church back there, Frank. The local belief was that the whole affair brought a curse on the parish and that nothing would ever prosper here again.

FRANK Jesus Christ, what a story! Jesus Christ, we don't know half of what goes on in the world!

TERRY (*To* TRISH) I'm sure that's the real reason why the pilgrimage out there really petered out. Couldn't have survived that.

TRISH Damn you, Terry Martin, how could you have brought us out to a place like that?

TERRY Trish, it is just an —

TRISH And how could you have bought an evil place like that?

TERRY The place is not evil, Trish.

TRISH I hate that story. That's a hateful story. You shouldn't have told us that story.

She moves quickly away and busies herself with her belongings. Silence.

BERNA (*To* FRANK) These grew. (*Her flowers*)

FRANK What's that?

BERNA He said nothing ever grew again. These did.

FRANK True . . . that's true . . . . Going to be another warm day.

TERRY Think so.

FRANK Yes. Very warm. Wonderful.

They all drift apart.

TRISH Shouldn't we tidy the place up a bit? Carlin could arrive any time.

BERNA You mean Charlie, don't you?

TRISH Do I? Whatever.

They begin tidying up, each attending to his/her own belongings. First they put on their shoes. Then TERRY *puts bottles, flasks, etc. back into the hampers.* TRISH *folds up sleeping-bags and packs her other belongings.* BERNA *folds her now dry clothes and puts them away.* FRANK *looks after his cameras, binoculars, etc.* ANGELA *makes a pile of the paper napkins, plastic cups, etc. scattered around the pier.* GEORGE *watches the others at their tasks. While all this tidying up is taking place, the following episodes happen:* BERNA *takes her scarf off the life-belt stand and puts it round her neck. Then she sees Angela's hat.*

BERNA   Isn't this your hat, Angela?
ANGELA Thanks.
BERNA   Do you want it?
ANGELA My good hat, for God's sake! Why wouldn't I want it? Thank you. The only sun hat I have.

> BERNA *hands the hat to* ANGELA. *A moment's hesitation. Then she removes the scarf from her neck and knots it on one of the arms of the stand.* FRANK *witnesses this episode.*

TRISH   (*To* GEORGE) I'll take that (*accordion*).
GEORGE Why?
TRISH   What d'you mean why? I'll put it in the case for you.
GEORGE Why?
TRISH   Because we're about to — Fine — fine! Suit yourself!
GEORGE Yes.

> TRISH *moves away from him.* FRANK *goes to the stand, takes off his belt and buckles it round the upright. Now he sees* TERRY *watching him.*

FRANK   (*Breezily*) Maybe that's a bit reckless, is it? D'you think they'll stay up by themselves?
TERRY   I'm all for a gamble.
FRANK   Pot belly. Safe enough.

TRISH *witnesses this episode. She looks at the mound of stones.*

TRISH Should we put these back where we found them?
BERNA I wouldn't bother. They were scattered all over the place when we got here.

TRISH goes to the stand. She takes off her bracelet and hangs it on one of the arms, balancing Berna's scarf. Then she goes back to GEORGE who is standing immobile beside their belongings.

TRISH Give me your handkerchief.

He does not move. TRISH takes the handkerchief out of his breast pocket, returns to the stand, and knots the handkerchief beside her bracelet.

ANGELA (*To TERRY*) Did you say you had honey cake?
TERRY Yes. Are you hungry?

He produces the cake from the hamper. A sealed tin.

How do you open this thing?
ANGELA No, no; don't open it. I'll leave it here, I think.

She places the tin on top of a bollard.

TERRY What are you doing?
ANGELA For Carlin. You don't mind, do you? He's sure to come snooping around after we've gone. A present.
TERRY Will you ever come back here?
ANGELA Just to keep him sweet.
BERNA Is this yours, Frank? (*Camera case*)
FRANK Just looking for that. Thank you.
ANGELA (*To TERRY*) Sorry for that outburst a while ago.
TERRY Please . . .
ANGELA It was a lovely birthday.
TERRY We'll not talk about that. Interesting place, though.
ANGELA Pretty.

TERRY   Wonderful, isn't it?

ANGELA   (*Gesturing to island*) I can live without all that stuff, Terry. Honestly. Housework — the kids — teaching — bills — Frank — doctors — more bills — just getting through every day is about as much as I can handle; more than I can handle at times. (*Remembering that the island is his*) I really wish you luck with it. Yes — yes — yes, of course it's wonderful — beautiful and wonderful.

TERRY   When will I see you?

ANGELA   Terry —

TERRY   Next Sunday?

ANGELA   No. Please.

> *She spreads her hands as if to say 'What's the point? Can't you see there's no point?' Then very quickly she takes his hands in hers, squeezes them, and then swiftly moves away from him.*
>   FRANK *has found a small bottle. He holds it up.*

FRANK   Anybody mind if I pour this out? (*Reads*) Cherry Brandy.

> *He empties it out.*

God, that's a sin, isn't it?

> *Now he picks up a plastic cup, scoops whatever water is left in the 'well', and pours it into the brandy bottle. Now he is aware that* TERRY *and* ANGELA *are watching him. He laughs.*

For a quick shot on the way home. In case Charlie's jokes get too bad. Hardly any (*water*) left . . .

> *He corks the bottle with paper tissues.* TRISH *goes to the small pile of rubbish (paper tissues, plastic cups, etc.) that* ANGELA *gathered. She strikes a match. Just as she is about to set fire to the refuse,* ANGELA *rushes to her and stamps the fire out with her foot.*

ANGELA For God's sake, woman!

TRISH What have I — ?

ANGELA You can't light a fire here! (*Calm again*) We can take this
away with us, can't we? That would be simpler,
wouldn't it?

And she begins piling the rubbish into a plastic bag.

TRISH (*Excessive astonishment*) Oh good Lord, we're suddenly
very house-proud, aren't we?

ANGELA *puts her hand on* TRISH's *elbow.*

ANGELA Sorry, Trish. Could do with some sleep.

*She moves away to the end of the pier and looks around.
The various tasks have been completed.*

FRANK Now, Terry. Yourself.

TERRY What's that?

FRANK You're going to leave a visiting card, aren't you?

TERRY A visiting — ?

FRANK On the stand. 'Terry Martin Was Here.'

TERRY (*Laughs*) Nothing to leave. (*Produces coins*) Is money
any good?

TRISH Useless, Terry.

TERRY What else can I give you?

FRANK What else can he give us? What about that shirt?

Suddenly everybody is listening, watching.

BERNA Yes, Terry. The shirt.

FRANK Is the shirt what we want?

TRISH The shirt will do.

BERNA We want the shirt!

TRISH Hand it over, Terry.

TERRY Ah, come on now —

FRANK We all want the shirt, don't we?

GEORGE Yes — yes — yes!

Now TRISH *sings rapidly — and keeps singing again and again, 'I want the shirt — I want the shirt', to the air of 'Here Comes the Bride'.*

FRANK We'll take it now, Terry.
BERNA We want it now, Terry, now.
TERRY Here — I'll give you a pen-knife — matches —
FRANK No good. The shirt, Terry. Hand it over.

      TERRY *tries to back away from them. They encircle him. They sing with* TRISH:

ALL 'We want the shirt — we want the shirt — '
TERRY My shoes! My shoes and socks —
BERNA The shirt, Terry.
TRISH The shirt — the shirt!
FRANK The shirt — the shirt — the shirt!

      ALL *sing again, 'We want the shirt — we want the shirt — '* GEORGE *plays 'Here Comes the Bride' and continues playing until after* FRANK's *'Pull — pull — pull!'*

TERRY For God's sake, this is the only shirt I have here!
FRANK Grab him!
TERRY Frank — !

      And suddenly they all grab him (all except ANGELA *who is by herself at the end of the pier — but watching).* TERRY *falls to the ground. They pull at his shirt. As they do, overlapping:*

BERNA We have him!
FRANK Hold his feet!
TERRY For God's sake!
TRISH Give it to us!
FRANK Hold him — hold him!
TRISH We want it — we want it!
TERRY Help!
BERNA Want it — want it — want it!
FRANK Want it, Terry — want it!

BERNA   Pull — pull — pull!

TRISH   I've got it!

BERNA   Rip it off!

TERRY   Angela, help — !

FRANK   Hold his hands!

BERNA   Need it — need it!

TRISH   Got it! Yes!

TERRY   Please — !

FRANK   Pull — pull — pull!

> *Now* FRANK *stands up in triumph, a portion of Terry's shirt held aloft.*

There!

TRISH   Well done, Frank.

BERNA   Now hang it up, Terry. (*To* ALL) Yes?

GEORGE   Yes — yes!

TRISH   Hang it up there, Terry. Come on — be a sport!

> TERRY *gets to his feet and pulls the remnant of his shirt together.*

TERRY   Happy now, are you?

FRANK   On the life-belt stand. Has to be done in person.

TERRY   You're a shower of bastards — you know that?

> *He takes the piece of the shirt and hangs it up. They applaud.*

BERNA   'Terry Martin Was Here.'

TERRY   Satisfied?

TRISH   Wonderful!

TERRY   Okay?

FRANK   You'll be remembered here forever, Terry.

TERRY   Happy now? I hope you're all happy now.

BERNA   Don't be such a crank.

FRANK   Bit of fun, Terry. That's all.

TERRY   (*Relenting*) Not a button left.

FRANK   Just passing the time — killing time.

TERRY   And I could have split my head on those stones!

FRANK Just a bit of fun.

FRANK goes to one of his bags and produces a shirt.

TRISH You look wonderful, Terry. Doesn't he?
FRANK This should fit you.

*TERRY raises his hand in a pretended gesture of striking
him.*

And it's your colour.
TERRY I like this now. I'm not going to part with it. Bastards . . .

*The moment has passed. They finish tidying up. They
look around the pier, now restored to what it was when
they arrived.*

TRISH So . . .
BERNA So . . .

*They look like people at a station — some standing,
some sitting — just waiting patiently to get away.*

TRISH Lovely harvest day, isn't it?
BERNA What time is it now?
FRANK Coming up to seven-thirty.

*Brief pause. FRANK sees two stones a few feet away
from the mound of stones. He picks one up and places it
on top of the mound.*

Simple domestic instincts . . .

*He now picks up the second stone and places it on top of
the mound.*

(*To* TERRY) At seven-thirty in the morning the rage for
the absolute isn't quite so consuming . . . . The acceptance of what *is* . . .

Brief pause.

ANGELA He's out there somewhere, just below the surface.
TERRY Who's that?
ANGELA His dancing porpoise.
FRANK Damn right. Waiting for an audience.
TERRY Not many audiences around here.
FRANK Or maybe just searching for the other thirteen. Who's to say?

Short pause.

TRISH Is he punctual?
TERRY (*Laughs*) Carlin?
TRISH (*Wearily*) God! Your driver — Charlie!
TERRY He'll be on time. He's always on bloody time.

Short pause.

TRISH (*To* GEORGE) Are you not going to put that into the case?
GEORGE No.
TRISH What's got into you?
GEORGE I'm not finished playing.

Short pause. ANGELA *is still by herself at the end of the pier.*

ANGELA There was a city called Eleusis in Attica in ancient Greece; and every year at the end of summer religious ceremonies were held there in honour of Demeter, the goddess of the harvest — what we would call a harvest festival. And they were known as the Eleusinian Mysteries.
FRANK Off again!
TRISH No more stories, Angela. Let's get back to real life.
ANGELA All we know about the ceremonies is that they began with a period of fasting; that there was a ritual purification in the sea; and that young people went through a ceremony of initiation. And there was music and

dancing and drinking. And we know, too, that sacrifice was offered. And that's about all we know. Because the people who took part in the ceremonies vowed never to speak of what happened there. So that when that civilisation came to an end it took the secrets of the Eleusinian Mysteries with it.

FRANK What's your point — that they had bishops too? I'll tell you something: it's going to be another roaster of a day.

Brief pause.

BERNA Play something for us, George.

GEORGE What?

BERNA Whatever gives you pleasure.

GEORGE My pleasure . . . right . . .

He strikes a few chords as he wonders what he will play. Then suddenly:

TRISH Shhh! Listen! Listen!

BERNA What is it?

TRISH Stop! Quiet! Stop!

FRANK Is it — ?

TRISH The minibus! Isn't it? Listen!

FRANK I don't hear —

BERNA It is! She's right!

TRISH At last! At last!

TERRY Told you he was bloody punctual.

They are all suddenly animated, excited, joyous. They pick up their belongings. They all talk at the same time.

FRANK Good old Charlie!

TERRY Who's is this?

TRISH What new jokes will he have?

ANGELA Don't forget your sleeping-bag.

BERNA We'll be home by lunch-time.

ANGELA Can you manage all that?

FRANK You're sun-burned.

GEORGE Am I?

FRANK Your forehead.

TRISH The moment I get home — straight to bed!

FRANK You're very lucky to have Charlie.

> *And gradually as the minibus gets closer, their chatter, and their excitement dies away. Now the minibus has arrived. The engine is switched off. FRANK goes to the exit.*

Good man, Charlie. With you in a moment.

> *He now sees the tin of honey cake and picks it up.*

What's this?

TERRY That's for Carlin.

FRANK Like hell. I'm taking —

TERRY Leave it, Frank.

FRANK Sorry . . .

> *Nobody moves, they look around. Nobody speaks. Finally:*

TRISH Nice place all the same . . . . Isn't it?

FRANK Lovely.

TRISH It really is, Terry.

BERNA So peaceful.

TRISH Lovely.

FRANK Really peaceful.

TRISH Wonderful.

FRANK Wonderful.

TRISH (*To* GEORGE) Isn't it wonderful?

GEORGE Yes.

TERRY Angela's right: it was a mess, the whole thing.

FRANK Terry —

TERRY The least said . . . . I just feel I've let you all down.

FRANK Don't say another word. It was a great birthday-party. We had a wonderful time.

TRISH He's right, Terry. Terrific.

FRANK Thank you. And we'll do it again some time. (*To* ALL)

Agreed? (*To* GEORGE) Right, George?

GEORGE *spreads his hands and smiles.*

Only this time I'll take Mr Carlin in hand and he'll do what he's supposed to do.
TRISH And even though we don't make it out there —
FRANK Of course we'll make it! Why wouldn't we make it?
TRISH Well at least now we know . . . it's there.
FRANK (*Calls*) 'Bye, Conall!
TRISH (*Calls*) 'Bye, Conall!

FRANK *sings 'Aloha'.*

TERRY I should tell you —
TRISH (*Calls*) Be good, Conall!
TERRY I should have said —
FRANK Trish, my love, you're looking nowhere near it.
TRISH What do you — ?

FRANK *turns her head to the right.*

FRANK Got it now?
TRISH Ah.
FRANK Still County Sligo.
TRISH I know it's County Sligo, Frank.
FRANK (*To* ALL) See? Nothing changes.
ANGELA (*To* TERRY) You should have told us what?
TERRY Nothing.
ANGELA What should you have told us?
TERRY (*Reluctantly*) What I said yesterday afternoon — this morning — I'm confused — when was it? — Anyhow, when I told you I owned the island, that *is* true — well partially true. I *have* taken an option on it. That option expires in a month. And I'm not going to pick it up.
TRISH Now that's the best news I've heard all day! The moment you told that story about —

TERRY *holds up his hand to silence her.*

TERRY I want to pick it up. Oh, yes. Trouble is — I haven't the money. The bookie business — concert promotion — the last few years have been disastrous. And I'm afraid — (*Laughs*) — not to put a tooth in it — I'm broke.

TRISH But, Terry, you —

TERRY Things will pick up. The tide will turn. I'll rise again. Oh, yes, I'll rise again. (*To* BERNA) That's why I didn't tell you I'd optioned it. Knew I'd lose it. (*To* ALL) Actually I didn't mean to tell anybody . . . Look at those solemn faces! (*Laughs*) To own Oileán Draíochta for four whole months — wasn't that wonderful enough? Wasn't that a terrific secret to have? Anyway . . . One small thing. I'd be glad if you kept it to yourselves — that I'm broke. Don't want a hundred creditors descending on me.

BERNA I'm sorry, Terry.

TERRY So we'll come back again, will we? What d'you say?

TRISH But, Terry, how can you — ?

TERRY When will we come back?

FRANK Good God, Terry, how can you?

TERRY Next year? What about next year?

FRANK If I'd known — if any of us had any idea you were —

TERRY My birthday next year — right?

FRANK And you've been doling out — day after day — month after —

ANGELA (*Triumphantly*) Yes, we will! Next year — and the year after — and the year after that! Because we want to! Not out of need — out of desire! Not in expectation — but to attest, to affirm, to acknowledge — to shout Yes, Yes, Yes! Damn right we will, Terry! Yes — yes — yes!

FRANK Twelve months time — agreed?

TRISH Agreed!

FRANK Berna?

BERNA Yes!

FRANK George?

GEORGE Agreed!

FRANK No more talk! Settled! (*Calls*) 'Bye, Conall! 'Bye, lads. They're waving to us! Wave back to them!

87

FRANK *waves vigorously.* TRISH, GEORGE *and* BERNA *make smaller gestures.*

TRISH 'Bye!

FRANK (*Calls*) Terry's birthday next year! And for a whole night!

They all join in, overlapping.

TRISH 'Bye, sheep!

GEORGE 'Bye.

TRISH 'Bye, cattle.

TERRY 'Bye, coloured birds.

BERNA 'Bye, whin bush.

FRANK 'Bye, bell.

TERRY 'Bye, clothes on bushes.

ANGELA 'Bye, low hill.

GEORGE 'Bye.

TRISH 'Bye, oak trees.

ANGELA 'Bye, apple trees.

TERRY 'Bye, Conall.

ALL 'Bye . . . 'bye . . . 'bye . . .

FRANK 'Bye, dancing dolphin . . . 'bye . . . 'bye . . .

Still nobody moves. Now GEORGE *plays in his 'sacred' style* 'Come, my love, come, my boat lies low, / She lies high and dry on the O-hi-o, / Come, my love, come, and come along with me / And I'll take you back to Tennessee'.

TRISH Charlie's waiting for us. Shouldn't we make a move?

But nobody moves. Now BERNA *begins to hum with the song, beginning with the first verse:*

BERNA 'Down by the cane-brake, close by the mill / There lived a blue-eyed girl and her name was Nancy Dill — '

GEORGE *accompanies her. Now* TERRY *hums with her. Together they hum:*

TERRY⎫ 'I told her that I loved her, I loved her very long, / I'm
BERNA⎭ going to serenade her and this will be my song . . . '

Now TRISH *and* FRANK *join in the humming: 'Come, my
love, come, my boat lies low, / She lies high and dry on
the O-hi-o, / Come my love, come, come along with me,
/ And I'll take you back to Tennessee —' They play/
hum another verse and this time* ANGELA *joins them.
(And this continues to the end of the play.)*

TRISH *goes to the mound of stones. She walks around
it once. Then she picks up a stone from the bottom of the
mound and places it on the top. Then she walks around
the mound a second time, and again she places a stone
on top. Then she goes to the life-belt stand and lightly
touches her votive offering. Then she goes to her
belongings, picks them up, and slowly moves off.*

The moment TRISH *completes her first encircling*
BERNA *joins her. First she places the flowers* FRANK
*gave her at the foot of the stand. Then she does the ritual
that* TRISH *is doing. And this ceremony — encircling,
lifting a stone, encircling, lifting a stone, touching the
votive offering — is repeated by every character.*
FRANK *immediately behind* BERNA, TERRY *immediately
after* FRANK. *And when they finish, they pick up their
belongings and — still humming to* GEORGE's *accompaniment — move slowly off. Now only* GEORGE *and*
ANGELA *are left.* GEORGE *stops playing. He looks at her
and gestures towards the mound.*

ANGELA You go ahead, George. I think I'll pass.

*She watches him as he does the ritual. When he has
finished he stands beside her, puts his arm on hers. They
take a last look round.*

GEORGE Nice place.
ANGELA Nice place.

She nods in agreement.

GEORGE You'll come back some day.

ANGELA I don't think —

GEORGE Yes, you will. Some day. And when you do, do it for me. No, no, I don't mean *for* me — just in memory of me.

She looks at him for a second. Then quickly, impetuously, she catches his head between her hands and kisses him. Then she breaks away from him, rushes to the stand, kisses her sun hat and hangs it resolutely on the very top of the stand.

ANGELA (*Defiantly*) For you, George! For both of us!

She rushes back to him, takes his arm and begins singing 'Down by the Cane-brake' loudly, joyously, happily — and he accompanies her with comparable brio. The others (off) join in.

GEORGE *and* ANGELA *exit. The engine starts up. The singing and the engine compete. Both sounds are encompassed by the silence and complete stillness and gradually surrender to it.*

Acknowledgements

The World is Waiting for the Sunrise Copyright © 1919, Chappell Music Ltd., London. Reproduced by permission of International Music Publications Ltd.

I Want to be Happy Copyright © 1920, Harms Inc., USA, Warner Chappell Music Ltd., London. Reproduced by permission of International Music Publications Ltd.

Jolly Good Company Copyright © 1931, Campbell, Connelly & Co. Ltd., 8-9 Frith Street, London W1V 5TZ. Used by permission, all rights reserved.

There Was I Waiting at the Church Copyright © 1906. Reproduced by permission of Francis Day and Hunter Ltd., London WC2H 0EA.

Down in de Cane-brake Copyright © 1928, Forster Music Pub Inc., USA. Reproduced by permission of Francis Day and Hunter Ltd., London WC2H 0EA.

Heavenly Sunshine Copyright © 1970, Al Gallico Music Corp., USA. Reproduced by permission of EMI Music Publishing Ltd., London WC2H 0EA.

Every effort has been made to contact all copyright holders of songs quoted in the text of this play. In case of any queries, please contact Curtis Brown Group Ltd., 162-168 Regent Street, London W1R 5TB.